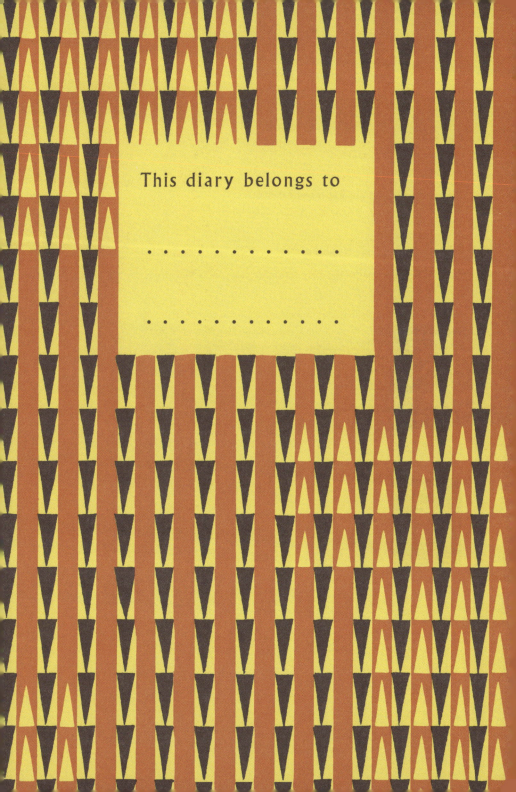

First published in 2008
by Faber and Faber Limited
3 Queen Square London WCIN 3AU

Designed and typeset by Faber and Faber Ltd
Printed in Italy by L.E.G.O S.p.A

All rights reserved
Selection and captions © Faber and Faber, 2008

Some of the captions for the diary are drawn from John Mullan's *Faber and Faber: A Publishing History*

United Kingdom calendarial information © Crown copyright
Reproduced by permission of the Controller of Her Majesty's Stationery Office and the UK Hydrographic Office (www.ukho.gov.uk)

Clauses in the Banking and Financial Dealings Act allow the Government to alter dates at short notice

A CIP record for this book
is available from the British Library

ISBN 978–0–571–24105–7

2 4 6 8 10 9 7 5 3 1

Faber and Faber Diary 2009

Faber and Faber was founded in 1929 . . .

. . . but its roots go back further to the Scientific Press, which started publishing in the early years of the century. The press was owned by Sir Maurice and Lady Gwyer, and their desire to expand into general publishing led them to Geoffrey Faber, a fellow of All Souls College, Oxford. Faber and Gwyer was founded in 1925. After four years Faber took the company forward alone, and the story goes that Walter de la Mare suggested adding a second, fictitious Faber to balance the company name.

In the meantime, the firm had prospered. T. S. Eliot, who had been suggested to Faber by a colleague at All Souls, had left Lloyds Bank in London to join him as a director, and in its first season the firm issued Eliot's *Poems 1909–1925*. In addition, the catalogues from the early years included books by Jean Cocteau, Herbert Read and Vita Sackville-West.

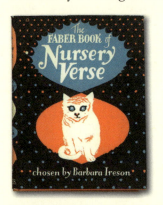

Poetry was always to be a significant element in the list and under Eliot's aegis W. H. Auden, Stephen Spender and Louis MacNeice soon joined Pound, Marianne Moore, Wyndham Lewis, James Joyce and Walter de la Mare.

Under Geoffrey Faber's chairmanship the board in 1929 included Eliot, Richard de la Mare, Charles Stewart and Frank Morley. This young team built up a comprehensive and profitable catalogue distinguished by distinctive design, much of which is still in print. Biographies, memoirs, fiction, poetry, political and religious essays, art and architecture monographs, children's books, and a pioneering range of ecology titles contributed towards an eclectic list full of character. Faber also produced Eliot's groundbreaking literary review the *Criterion*.

The Second World War brought both paper shortages and higher taxes, and the post-war years continued to be difficult. However, as the economy recovered a

new generation of writers joined Faber, including William Golding, Lawrence Durrell, Robert Lowell, Ted Hughes, Sylvia Plath, Philip Larkin and P. D. James. Tom Stoppard and John Osborne were also added, representing the firm's growing commitment to modern drama.

The 1970s and 1980s saw a blossoming in literary fiction, with the addition of authors such as Peter Carey, Kazuo Ishiguro, Mario Vargas Llosa, Milan Kundera and Garrison Keillor.

The year 2009 finds the publishing company that Geoffrey Faber founded remaining true to the principles he instigated and independent of corporate ownership. In its eighty years of publishing, Faber can count among its authors six Booker Prize winners (and numerous shortlistings), fifteen Whitbread Award winners, seven Forward Poetry Prize winners and eleven Nobel Laureates.

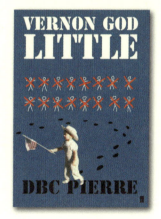

In addition to dedicated core publishing, recent years have seen some new strands emerge, including a distinctive Faber audio list and the launch of Faber Finds, an imprint that employs print-on-demand technology to bring great works of literature back to life.

Although this diary can show only a fraction of the books that have shaped the company's fortunes and reputation over the years, it is dedicated to all the authors, illustrators and readers who have created, worked on, or enjoyed the many thousands of titles published under the distinctive Faber and Faber imprint since 1929.

ANNUAL CALENDARS 2009

JANUARY
M	T	W	T	F	S	S
29	30	31	1	2	3	4
5	6	7	8	9	10	11
12	13	14	15	16	17	18
19	20	21	22	23	24	25
26	27	28	29	30	31	1
2	3	4	5	6	7	8

FEBRUARY
M	T	W	T	F	S	S
26	27	28	29	30	31	1
2	3	4	5	6	7	8
9	10	11	12	13	14	15
16	17	18	19	20	21	22
23	24	25	26	27	28	1
2	3	4	5	6	7	8

MARCH
M	T	W	T	F	S	S
23	24	25	26	27	28	1
2	3	4	5	6	7	8
9	10	11	12	13	14	15
16	17	18	19	20	21	22
23	24	25	26	27	28	29
30	31	1	2	3	4	5

APRIL
M	T	W	T	F	S	S
30	31	1	2	3	4	5
6	7	8	9	10	11	12
13	14	15	16	17	18	19
20	21	22	23	24	25	26
27	28	29	30	1	2	3

MAY
M	T	W	T	F	S	S
27	28	29	30	1	2	3
4	5	6	7	8	9	10
11	12	13	14	15	16	17
18	19	20	21	22	23	24
25	26	27	28	29	30	31

JUNE
M	T	W	T	F	S	S
1	2	3	4	5	6	7
8	9	10	11	12	13	14
15	16	17	18	19	20	21
22	23	24	25	26	27	28
29	30	1	2	3	4	5

JULY
M	T	W	T	F	S	S
29	30	1	2	3	4	5
6	7	8	9	10	11	12
13	14	15	16	17	18	19
20	21	22	23	24	25	26
27	28	29	30	31	1	2
3	4	5	6	7	8	9

AUGUST
M	T	W	T	F	S	S
28	28	29	30	31	1	2
3	4	5	6	7	8	9
10	11	12	13	14	15	16
17	18	19	20	21	22	23
24	25	26	27	28	29	30
31	1	2	3	4	5	6

SEPTEMBER
M	T	W	T	F	S	S
31	1	2	3	4	5	6
7	8	9	10	11	12	13
14	15	16	17	18	19	20
21	22	23	24	25	26	27
28	29	30	1	2	3	4
5	6	7	8	9	10	11

OCTOBER
M	T	W	T	F	S	S
28	29	30	1	2	3	4
5	6	7	8	9	10	11
12	13	14	15	16	17	18
19	20	21	22	23	24	25
26	27	28	29	30	31	1
2	3	4	5	6	7	8

NOVEMBER
M	T	W	T	F	S	S
26	27	28	29	30	31	1
2	3	4	5	6	7	8
9	10	11	12	13	14	15
16	17	18	19	20	21	22
23	24	25	26	27	28	29
30	1	2	3	4	5	6

DECEMBER
M	T	W	T	F	S	S
30	1	2	3	4	5	6
7	8	9	10	11	12	13
14	15	16	17	18	19	20
21	22	23	24	25	26	27
28	29	30	31	1	2	3
4	5	6	7	8	9	10

2008

JANUARY
M	T	W	T	F	S	S
31	1	2	3	4	5	6
7	8	9	10	11	12	13
14	15	16	17	18	19	20
21	22	23	24	25	26	27
28	29	30	31	1	2	3
4	5	6	7	8	9	10

FEBRUARY
M	T	W	T	F	S	S
28	29	30	31	1	2	3
4	5	6	7	8	9	10
11	12	13	14	15	16	17
18	19	20	21	22	23	24
25	26	27	28	29	1	2
3	4	5	6	7	8	9

MARCH
M	T	W	T	F	S	S
25	26	27	28	29	1	2
3	4	5	6	7	8	9
10	11	12	13	14	15	16
17	18	19	20	21	22	23
24	25	26	27	28	29	30
31	1	2	3	4	5	6

APRIL
M	T	W	T	F	S	S
31	1	2	3	4	5	6
7	8	9	10	11	12	13
14	15	16	17	18	19	20
21	22	23	24	25	26	27
28	29	30	1	2	3	4
5	6	7	8	9	10	11

MAY
M	T	W	T	F	S	S
28	29	30	1	2	3	4
5	6	7	8	9	10	11
12	13	14	15	16	17	18
19	20	21	22	23	24	25
26	27	28	29	30	31	1
2	3	4	5	6	7	8

JUNE
M	T	W	T	F	S	S
26	27	28	29	30	31	1
2	3	4	5	6	7	8
9	10	11	12	13	14	15
16	17	18	19	20	21	22
23	24	25	26	27	28	29
30	1	2	3	4	5	6

JULY
M	T	W	T	F	S	S
30	1	2	3	4	5	6
7	8	9	10	11	12	13
14	15	16	17	18	19	20
21	22	23	24	25	26	27
28	29	30	31	1	2	3
4	5	6	7	8	9	10

AUGUST
M	T	W	T	F	S	S
28	29	30	31	1	2	3
4	5	6	7	8	9	10
11	12	13	14	15	16	17
18	19	20	21	22	23	24
25	26	27	28	29	30	31
1	2	3	4	5	6	7

SEPTEMBER
M	T	W	T	F	S	S
1	2	3	4	5	6	7
8	9	10	11	12	13	14
15	16	17	18	19	20	21
22	23	24	25	26	27	28
29	30	1	2	3	4	5

OCTOBER
M	T	W	T	F	S	S
29	30	1	2	3	4	5
6	7	8	9	10	11	12
13	14	15	16	17	18	19
20	21	22	23	24	25	26
27	28	29	30	31	1	2

NOVEMBER
M	T	W	T	F	S	S
27	28	29	30	31	1	2
3	4	5	6	7	8	9
10	11	12	13	14	15	16
17	18	19	20	21	22	23
24	25	26	27	28	29	30

DECEMBER
M	T	W	T	F	S	S
1	2	3	4	5	6	7
8	9	10	11	12	13	14
15	16	17	18	19	20	21
22	23	24	25	26	27	28
29	30	31	1	2	3	4

2010

JANUARY
M	T	W	T	F	S	S
28	29	30	31	1	2	3
4	5	6	7	8	9	10
11	12	13	14	15	16	17
18	19	20	21	22	23	24
25	26	27	28	29	30	31

FEBRUARY
M	T	W	T	F	S	S
1	2	3	4	5	6	7
8	9	10	11	12	13	14
15	16	17	18	19	20	21
22	23	24	25	26	27	28
1	2	3	4	5	6	7

MARCH
M	T	W	T	F	S	S
1	2	3	4	5	6	7
8	9	10	11	12	13	14
15	16	17	18	19	20	21
22	23	24	25	26	27	28
29	30	31	1	2	3	4

APRIL
M	T	W	T	F	S	S
29	30	31	1	2	3	4
5	6	7	8	9	10	11
12	13	14	15	16	17	18
19	20	21	22	23	24	25
26	27	28	29	30	1	2

MAY
M	T	W	T	F	S	S
26	27	28	29	30	1	2
3	4	5	6	7	8	9
10	11	12	13	14	15	16
17	18	19	20	21	22	23
24	25	26	27	28	29	30
31	1	2	3	4	5	6

JUNE
M	T	W	T	F	S	S
31	1	2	3	4	5	6
7	8	9	10	11	12	13
14	15	16	17	18	19	20
21	22	23	24	25	26	27
28	29	30	1	2	3	4
5	6	7	8	9	10	11

JULY
M	T	W	T	F	S	S
28	29	30	1	2	3	4
5	6	7	8	9	10	11
12	13	14	15	16	17	18
19	20	21	22	23	24	25
26	27	28	29	30	31	1
2	3	4	5	6	7	8

AUGUST
M	T	W	T	F	S	S
26	27	28	29	30	31	1
2	3	4	5	6	7	8
9	10	11	12	13	14	15
16	17	18	19	20	21	22
23	24	25	26	27	28	29
30	31	1	2	3	4	5

SEPTEMBER
M	T	W	T	F	S	S
30	31	1	2	3	4	5
6	7	8	9	10	11	12
13	14	15	16	17	18	19
20	21	22	23	24	25	26
27	28	29	30	1	2	3

OCTOBER
M	T	W	T	F	S	S
27	28	29	30	1	2	3
4	5	6	7	8	9	10
11	12	13	14	15	16	17
18	19	20	21	22	23	24
25	26	27	28	29	30	31

NOVEMBER
M	T	W	T	F	S	S
1	2	3	4	5	6	7
8	9	10	11	12	13	14
15	16	17	18	19	20	21
22	23	24	25	26	27	28
29	30	1	2	3	4	5

DECEMBER
M	T	W	T	F	S	S
29	30	1	2	3	4	5
6	7	8	9	10	11	12
13	14	15	16	17	18	19
20	21	22	23	24	25	26
27	28	29	30	31	1	2

'My childhood was a queer and not altogether happy one.'

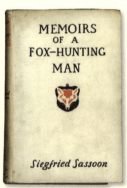

The lead item in Faber's inaugural catalogue was Siegfried Sassoon's *Memoirs of a Fox-Hunting Man*, which depicts the coming of age of the semi-autobiographical George Sherston. First published anonymously the previous year, it now came with its author's name declared in an edition handsomely illustrated by William Nicholson. The catalogue was able to pronounce it 'already a classic', and six months after its first appearance it was being reprinted for the eighth time. Sassoon was to publish two further volumes to complete the Sherston Trilogy as well as establishing himself as a key twentieth-century poet.

DECEMBER 2008 / JANUARY 2009

29 Monday

30 Tuesday

31 Wednesday

1 Thursday NEW YEAR'S DAY (GB, IRL, CA, AU, ZA)

2 Friday NEW YEAR HOLIDAY (SCT)

3 Saturday   **4** Sunday

'The sea is high again today, with a thrilling flush of wind.'

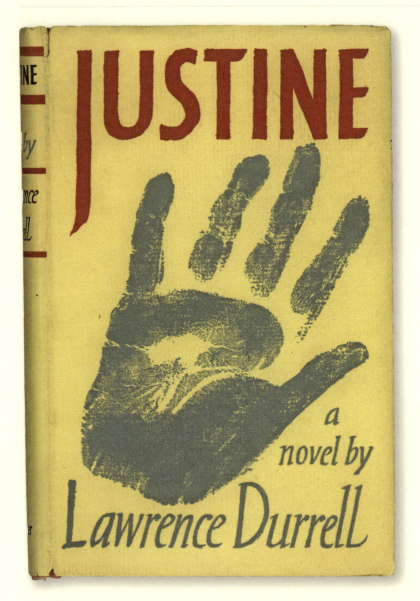

Justine, the first volume in Lawrence Durrell's Alexandria Quartet, was published in 1958. Radical in form and sensually lyrical, the quartet is a cornerstone of the modern novel. The designer of the cover, Berthold Wolpe, worked on Faber books for thirty years and created a distinctive house style based on lettering and plain colours. The handprint was made by Wolpe's daughter, Sarah.

JANUARY 2009

5 Monday

6 Tuesday

7 Wednesday

8 Thursday

9 Friday

10 Saturday   **11** Sunday

'Larkin lived a much more dramatic and intense life than he let on . . .'

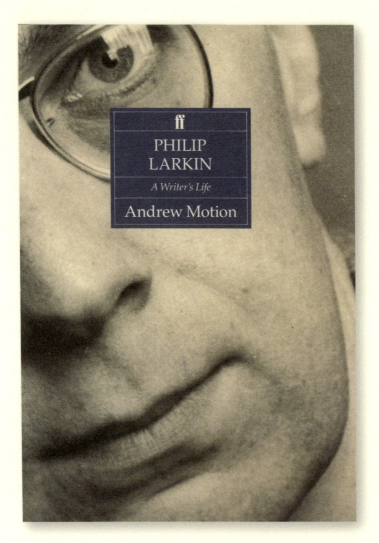
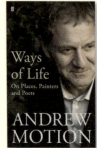
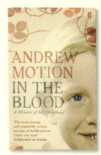
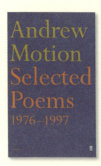

Andrew Motion's prize-winning biography of Philip Larkin revealed the poet in the round. Following shortly on from Faber's publication of Larkin's *Selected Letters*, it was the literary sensation of the early 1990s. Motion was appointed Poet Laureate in 1999, and his long and vital association with Faber encompasses anthologies, volumes of poetry, biographies, a novella and a memoir. His collection of essays *Ways of Life* was published in 2008.

JANUARY 2009

12 Monday

13 Tuesday

14 Wednesday

15 Thursday

16 Friday

17 Saturday   **18** Sunday

Don Paterson

Waking with Russell

Whatever the difference is, it all began
the day we woke up face-to-face like lovers
and his four-day-old smile dawned on him again,
possessed him, till it would not fall or waver;
and I pitched back not my old hard-pressed grin
but his own smile, or one I'd rediscovered.
Dear son, I was *mezzo del cammin*
and the true path was as lost to me as ever
when you cut in front and lit it as you ran.
See how the true gift never leaves the giver:
returned and redelivered, it rolled on
until the smile poured through us like a river.
How fine, I thought, this waking amongst men!
I kissed your mouth and pledged myself forever.

JANUARY 2009

19 Monday

Don Paterson
Landing Light

20 Tuesday

21 Wednesday

22 Thursday

23 Friday

24 Saturday				**25** Sunday BURNS NIGHT

'The Iron Man came to the top of the cliff. How far had he walked? Nobody knows.'

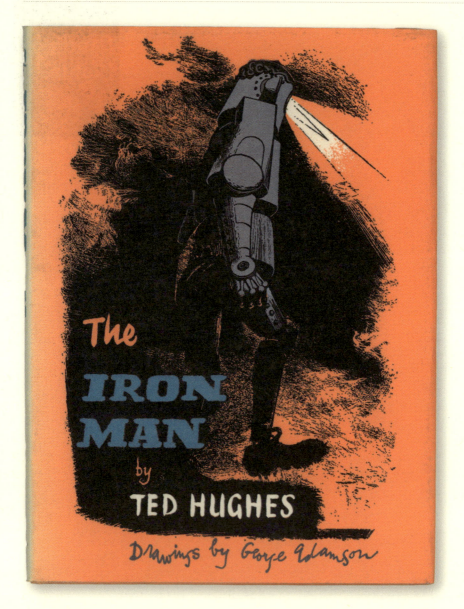

In 1961 Faber published the celebrated poet Ted Hughes's first book for children, *Meet My Folks*. His bestselling work *The Iron Man* followed in 1968 and has entertained generations of children since, selling over a million copies in the United Kingdom alone. *The Iron Woman* was published in 1993.

JANUARY/FEBRUARY 2009

26 Monday AUSTRALIA DAY (AU)

27 Tuesday

28 Wednesday

29 Thursday

30 Friday

31 Saturday   **1** Sunday

'I occasionally dream of Faber & Faber – music publishers!'

> Thank you so much for the Larkin. It is a moving poem indeed. By a coincidence Peter brought a volume of his verse out here, which I am now going to look at properly.
>
> I must stop this drivel – too long already – & go for a walk, have a look at a favourite church, & then back to the 'river.'
>
> Love to you all, & don't worry too much about – Y –, I'm sure there'll be some future. I occasionally dream of Faber & Faber – music publishers!
>
> Yours ever
> Ben

When Benjamin Britten was thinking of parting company with his publisher of nearly thirty years, he mentioned the idea of Faber Music as an aside to musicologist Donald Mitchell. When T. S. Eliot heard of the proposal, he declared, 'I have no idea how this can be done, but clearly we have to do it.' Thus began, in 1965, the separate company of Faber Music Ltd, specialising in the publication of sheet music. Britten became one of Faber Music's board members, and Donald Mitchell its Managing Director.

FEBRUARY 2009

2 Monday

3 Tuesday

4 Wednesday

5 Thursday

6 Friday WAITANGI DAY (NZ)

7 Saturday

8 Sunday

'Exactly three months before the killing at Martingale Mrs Maxie gave a dinner party.'

Faber published P. D. James's first book, *Cover Her Face*, in 1962. James, who was working full-time as a hospital administrator and writing in the evenings, was looking for a publisher. Her agent Elaine Greene happened to sit next to Faber Editorial Director Charles Monteith at a dinner at an Oxford college. Monteith was bemoaning the absence of new blood in Faber's crime list. Greene offered him her fresh manuscript and a relationship was born that has lasted over forty years and seventeen novels. *The Private Patient* was published in 2008.

FEBRUARY 2009

9 Monday

10 Tuesday

11 Wednesday

12 Thursday

13 Friday

14 Saturday ST VALENTINE'S DAY   **15** Sunday

Sylvia Plath

Sheep in Fog

The hills step off into whiteness.
People or stars
Regard me sadly, I disappoint them.

The train leaves a line of breath.
O slow
Horse the color of rust,

Hooves, dolorous bells –
All morning the
Morning has been blackening,

A flower left out.
My bones hold a stillness, the far
Fields melt my heart.

They threaten
To let me through to a heaven
Starless and fatherless, a dark water.

FEBRUARY 2009

16 Monday

17 Tuesday

18 Wednesday

19 Thursday

20 Friday

21 Saturday   22 Sunday

'The Naming of Cats is a difficult matter . . .'

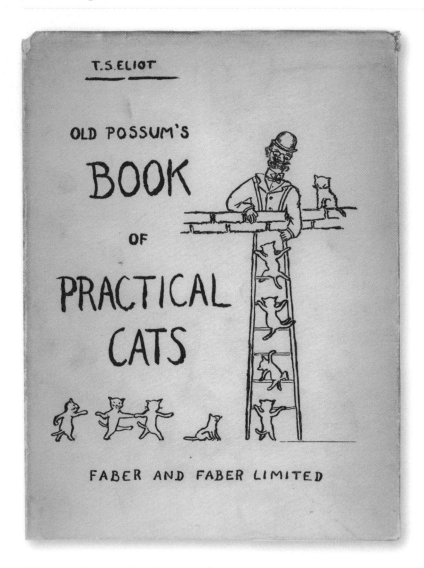

The jacket of the 1939 first edition of *Old Possum's Book of Practical Cats* was illustrated by Eliot himself. Nicolas Bentley and Edward Gorey produced drawings for much-loved editions in 1940 and 1982. In 1981 Andrew Lloyd Webber adapted some of the poems into the hit musical *Cats*, which continues to play around the world. This year a new generation of children will discover Rumpelteazer, Skimbleshanks, Mr Mistoffelees et al. in a special edition illustrated by Axel Scheffler, whose work includes *The Gruffalo*.

FEBRUARY/MARCH 2009

23 Monday

24 Tuesday PANCAKE DAY

25 Wednesday

26 Thursday

27 Friday

28 Saturday

1 Sunday ST DAVID'S DAY

'The idea of eternal return is a mysterious one...'

'A dark and brilliant achievement.' Ian McEwan

The 1980s, under the editorship of Robert McCrum, saw Faber fiction take on an international character. Unlike Kundera's most recent works, *The Unbearable Lightness of Being* was originally written in Czech. Acclaimed on its publication in 1984, it has reached the status of a modern classic and endures as one of his best-loved and most widely read novels. Kundera also provided the cover illustration.

MARCH 2009

2 Monday LABOUR DAY (AU)

3 Tuesday

4 Wednesday

5 Thursday

6 Friday

7 Saturday **8** Sunday

'In the end, / the water was too cold for us.'

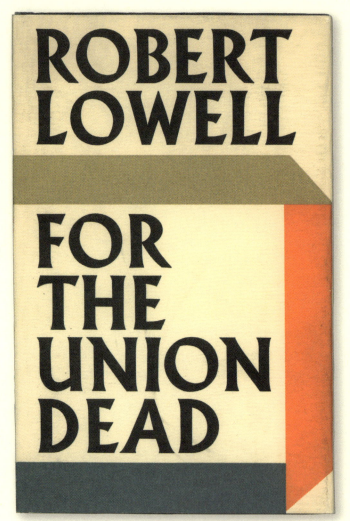
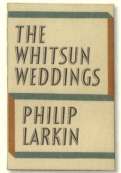

The sixties began with new volumes from W. H. Auden, Ezra Pound, E. E. Cummings and John Berryman, with the landmark volume *Selected Poems* jointly authored by Thom Gunn and Ted Hughes appearing in 1962. Philip Larkin's relationship with the company dated back to the 1940s, but it was not until 1964 that his first collection for Faber, *The Whitsun Weddings*, was published. In that same year, *For the Union Dead* demonstrated the ever-widening influence of Robert Lowell's new confessional style. *Ariel*, Sylvia Plath's posthumous collection, appeared in 1965.

MARCH 2009

9 Monday COMMONWEALTH DAY

10 Tuesday

11 Wednesday

12 Thursday

13 Friday

14 Saturday

15 Sunday

Ezra Pound

In a Station of the Metro

The apparition of these faces in the crowd;
Petals on a wet, black bough.

MARCH 2009

16 Monday

17 Tuesday ST PATRICK'S DAY (IRL, NIR)

18 Wednesday

19 Thursday

20 Friday

21 Saturday HUMAN RIGHTS DAY (ZA) **22** Sunday UK MOTHERING SUNDAY

Film-makers on film-making

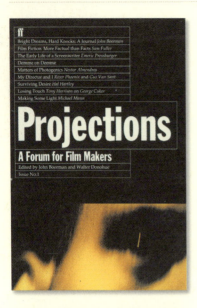

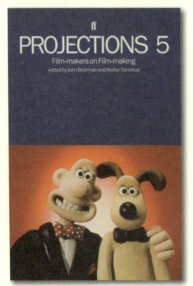

Now available online, *Projections* has established itself as a unique space for film-makers to write seriously about their craft and to dream about what movies can be. It was devised by long-time collaborators Walter Donohue and film director John Boorman as despatches from the front by practitioners in the film industry.

MARCH 2009

23 Monday

24 Tuesday

25 Wednesday

26 Thursday

27 Friday

28 Saturday

29 Sunday   BRITISH SUMMER TIME BEGINS

Simon Armitage

The Spelling

I left a spelling at my father's house
written in small coins on his front step.
It said which star I was heading for next,
which channel to watch, which button to press.
I should have waited, given that spelling
a voice, but I was handsome and late.

While I was gone he replied with pebbles
and leaves at my gate. But a storm got up
from the west, sluicing all meaning and shape.

I keep his broken spelling in a tin,
tip it out on the cellar floor, hoping
a letter or even a word will form.
And I am all grief, staring through black space
to meet his eyes, trying to read his face.

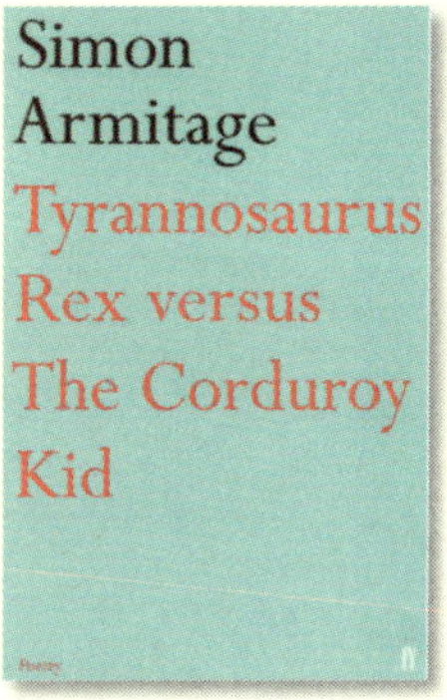

MARCH/APRIL 2009

30 Monday

Simon Armitage
Tyrannosaurus Rex versus The Corduroy Kid

31 Tuesday

1 Wednesday

2 Thursday

3 Friday

4 Saturday

5 Sunday

'I'm inclined to think we ought to take this man now. Let's discuss him.'

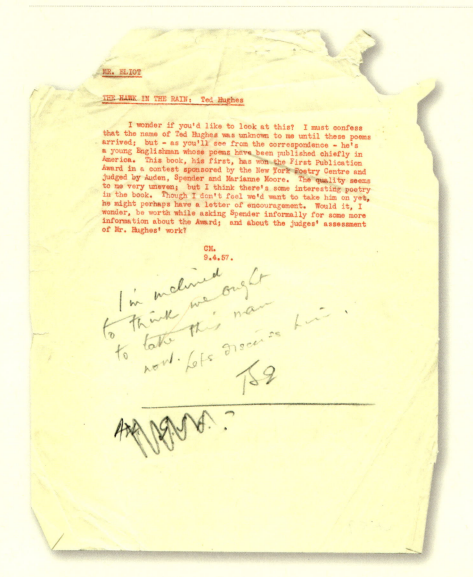

From the Faber Archive, dated 9 April 1957. Published in the same year, Ted Hughes's first collection, *The Hawk in the Rain*, was followed by many volumes of poetry and prose for adults and children. He was Poet Laureate from 1984, and in 1998 was appointed to the Order of Merit. His death in 1998 was a national event, made all the more so by the publication of *Birthday Letters* only months before. It won the Forward Poetry Prize, the T. S. Eliot Prize and the Whitbread Book of the Year Award.

APRIL 2009

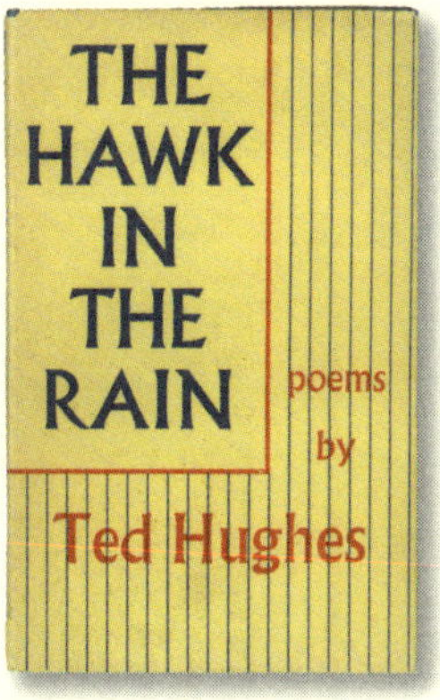

6 Monday

7 Tuesday

8 Wednesday

9 Thursday

10 Friday GOOD FRIDAY (GB, CA, AU, ZA)

11 Saturday EASTER SATURDAY (AU)   **12** Sunday EASTER SUNDAY

'It was a wrong number that started it . . .'

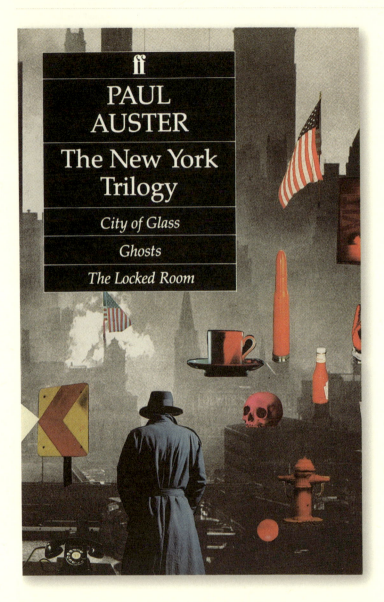

In 1987 Faber published *The New York Trilogy* by the then almost unknown American writer Paul Auster. Seen as both a gripping thriller and a masterclass in postmodernist technique, *The New York Trilogy* became a major bestseller. Auster has gone on to publish screenplays, poems and a further twelve novels with Faber, most recently *Man in the Dark* in 2008.

APRIL 2009

13 Monday   EASTER MONDAY (GB, CA, AU, ZA)

14 Tuesday

15 Wednesday

16 Thursday

17 Friday

18 Saturday   **19** Sunday

Paul Muldoon

The Boundary Commission

You remember that village where the border ran
Down the middle of the street,
With the butcher and baker in different states?
Today he remarked how a shower of rain

Had stopped so cleanly across Golightly's lane
It might have been a wall of glass
That had toppled over. He stood there, for ages,
To wonder which side, if any, he should be on.

APRIL 2009

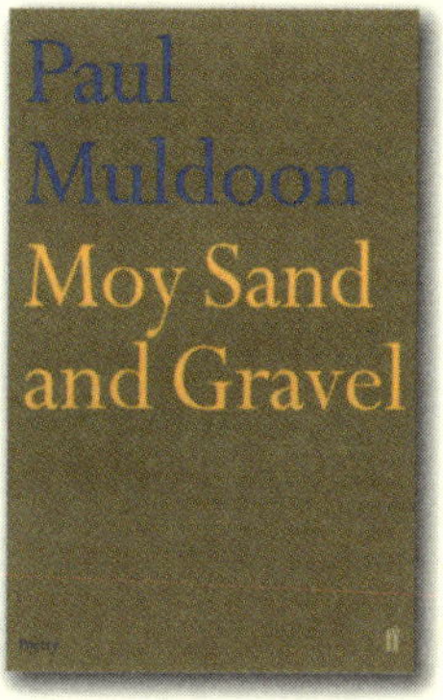

20 Monday

21 Tuesday

22 Wednesday

23 Thursday ST GEORGE'S DAY

24 Friday

25 Saturday ANZAC DAY (AU, NZ)   **26** Sunday

'It was a queer, sultry summer, the summer they electrocuted the Rosenbergs . . .'

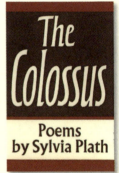

The Bell Jar was first published in 1963, the year of Sylvia Plath's death, under the pseudonym Victoria Lucas. Reissued in 1966 under Plath's own name, it has become a modern classic. Plath's first poetry collection, *The Colossus*, was published in 1960, followed by the posthumous publication of *Ariel* (edited by her husband, Ted Hughes) in 1965, *Crossing the Water* and *Winter Trees* in 1971, *The Collected Poems of Sylvia Plath* in 1981, and *The Journals of Sylvia Plath* in 2000. In 2004 Faber published *Ariel: The Restored Edition*, which reinstated Plath's original choice and order of poems.

APRIL/MAY 2009

27 Monday FREEDOM DAY (ZA)

28 Tuesday

29 Wednesday

30 Thursday

1 Friday WORKERS' DAY (ZA)

2 Saturday

3 Sunday

Alan Bennett

2 January. I'm sent a complimentary [sic] copy of Waterstone's Literary Diary which records the birthdays of various contemporary figures from the world of letters. Here is Dennis Potter on 17 May, Michael Frayn on 8 September, Edna O'Brien on 15 December, and so naturally I turn to my own birthday. May 9 is blank except for the note: 'The first British self-service launderette is opened on Queensway, London 1949.'

Untold Stories

 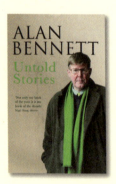 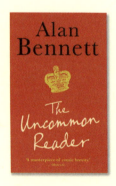

Alan Bennett's plays have been published by Faber since the 1960s and include *Forty Years On*, *The Lady in the Van* and *The History Boys*. Faber's bestseller of the 1990s was Bennett's collection of prose *Writing Home* (1994), which was followed by *Untold Stories* in 2005. His novella *The Uncommon Reader* was published in 2007.

MAY 2009

4 Monday MAY DAY (GB, IRL)

5 Tuesday

6 Wednesday

7 Thursday

8 Friday

9 Saturday   **10** Sunday

'My name is Karim Amir, and I am an Englishman born and bred, almost.'

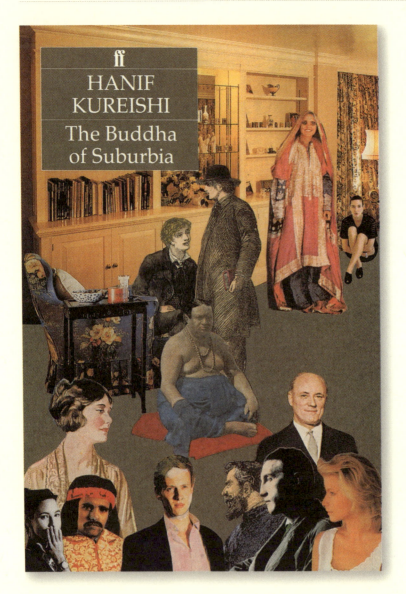

Hanif Kureishi's 1990 modern *Bildungsroman*, *The Buddha of Suburbia*, broke new ground in portraying the Anglo-Indian experience of the 1970s, making Kureishi a household name. He has gone on to forge a formidable literary reputation, and his most recent novel, *Something to Tell You*, was published to great acclaim in 2008.

MAY 2009

11 Monday

12 Tuesday

13 Wednesday

14 Thursday

15 Friday

16 Saturday   **17** Sunday

Alice Oswald

Leaf

For J.O. and L.O.

the leaf that now lies being made
in its shell of scale, the hush of things
unseen inside, the heartbeat of dead wood.
the slow through-flow that feeds
a form curled under, hour by hour
the thick reissuing starlike shapes
of cells and pores and water-rods
which builds up, which becomes a pressure,
a gradual fleshing out of a longing for light,
a small hand unfolding, feeling about.
into that hand the entire
object of the self being coldly placed,
the provisional, the inexplicable I
in mid-air, meeting the wind and dancing

MAY 2009

18 Monday VICTORIA DAY (CA)

19 Tuesday

20 Wednesday

21 Thursday

22 Friday

23 Saturday   **24** Sunday

'I am nothing but a corpse now, a body at the bottom of a well.'

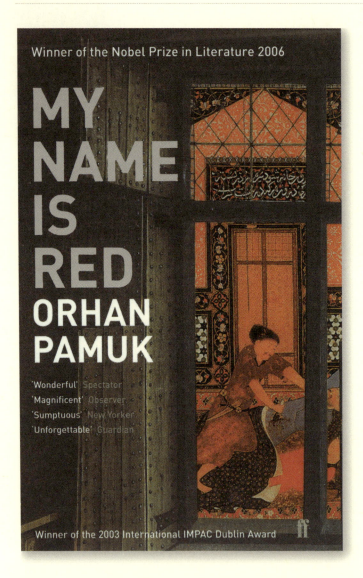

Already a tremendously popular author in Turkey, Orhan Pamuk achieved international success with his great historical novel *My Name Is Red*. A bravura piece of storytelling, this novel won the IMPAC Prize, and was followed by *Snow* and his memoir *Istanbul*. In presenting Pamuk with the Nobel Prize, the Swedish Academy celebrated his achievement as a writer 'who in the quest for the melancholic soul of his native city has discovered new symbols for the clash and interlacing of cultures'.

MAY 2009

25 Monday   SPRING BANK HOLIDAY (GB)

26 Tuesday

27 Wednesday

28 Thursday

29 Friday

30 Saturday   **31** Sunday

Faber drama: Osborne, Friel and Stoppard

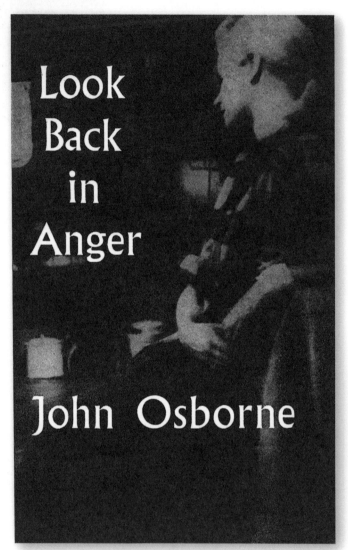

In 1957, John Osborne's theatrical bombshell *Look Back in Anger* launched the drama list in earnest. *Philadelphia Here I Come!* in 1964, saw Brian Friel established as the heir of such distinguished predecessors as Yeats, Synge, O'Casey and Beckett. Tom Stoppard joined the list in 1967 after causing a sensation at the Edinburgh Festival with *Rosencrantz and Guildenstern Are Dead*.

JUNE 2009

1 Monday JUNE BANK HOLIDAY (IRL), QUEEN'S BIRTHDAY HOLIDAY (NZ)

ROSEN-
CRANTZ
and
GUILDEN-
STERN
are DEAD
by Tom
Stoppard

2 Tuesday

3 Wednesday

4 Thursday

5 Friday

6 Saturday   **7** Sunday

'It seems increasingly likely that I really will undertake the expedition . . .'

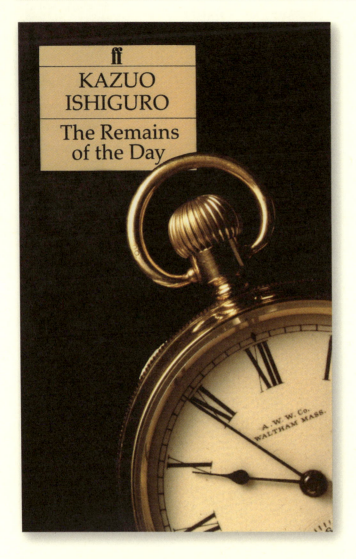

The Remains of the Day won the Booker Prize in 1989. A beautiful and haunting evocation of life between the wars in a great English house, of lost causes and lost love, it was later made into an acclaimed film by Merchant Ivory. Ishiguro's other novels are *A Pale View of Hills*, *An Artist of the Floating World*, *The Unconsoled*, *When We Were Orphans* and *Never Let Me Go*. He received an OBE for Services to Literature in 1995, and the French decoration of Chevalier de l'Ordre des Arts et des Lettres in 1998. *Nocturnes* will be published this year.

JUNE 2009

8 Monday QUEEN'S BIRTHDAY HOLIDAY (AU, NZ)

9 Tuesday

10 Wednesday

11 Thursday

12 Friday

13 Saturday   **14** Sunday

Marianne Moore

A Jelly-Fish

Visible, invisible,
A fluctuating charm,
An amber-colored amethyst
Inhabits it; your arm
Approaches, and
It opens and
It closes;
You have meant
To catch it,
And it shrivels;
You abandon
Your intent –
It opens, and it
Closes and you
Reach for it –
The blue
Surrounding it
Grows cloudy, and
It floats away
From you.

JUNE 2009

15 Monday

16 Tuesday YOUTH DAY (ZA)

17 Wednesday

18 Thursday

19 Friday

20 Saturday

21 Sunday UK FATHERS' DAY

'A historical grammar of the language of poetic myth.'

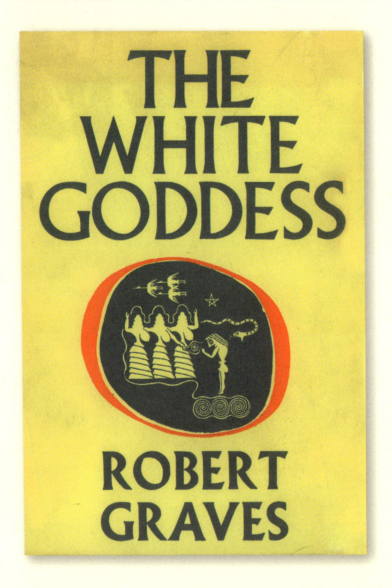

In 1948, Faber published *The White Goddess* by Robert Graves: 'a true follower of Aeneas into the nether world' (as the catalogue put it). The influence of Graves's extraordinary recasting of European myth – 'prodigious, monstrous, stupefying, indescribable' – is to be seen in the work of many other poets, several published by Faber, including Auden, MacNeice, Hughes and Heaney.

JUNE 2009

22 Monday

23 Tuesday

24 Wednesday

25 Thursday

26 Friday

27 Saturday   **28** Sunday

'When Eddie Dickens was eleven years old, both his parents caught some awful disease . . .'

Throughout the 1990s the Faber children's list continued to grow both in reputation and in the eclecticism of its publishing. As well as being the established home of much-loved children's classics, Faber was discovering and making famous new and truly exceptional writers of children's literature. In 2000, Faber published the first of Philip Ardagh's Eddie Dickens Trilogy, *Awful End*, with illustrations by David Roberts. The Eddie Dickens Trilogy and two further trilogies have now been translated into over thirty languages.

JUNE/JULY 2009

29 Monday

30 Tuesday

1 Wednesday CANADA DAY (CA)

2 Thursday

3 Friday

4 Saturday

5 Sunday

Faber drama: Hampton, Hare and Wertenbaker

Christopher Hampton joined Faber in 1967 when, with the transfer from the Royal Court Theatre of his play *When Did You Last See My Mother?*, he became the youngest writer ever to have a play in the West End. In 1971, Faber published David Hare's *Slag*, a play reflecting the energies of a new generation of British dramatists. Timberlake Wertenbaker, one of the first women on the list, came to Faber in 1984 with *New Anatomies*, which was soon followed by *The Grace of Mary Traverse*.

JULY 2009

6 Monday

7 Tuesday

8 Wednesday

9 Thursday

10 Friday

11 Saturday   **12** Sunday

'Imagine a ruin so strange it must never have happened.'

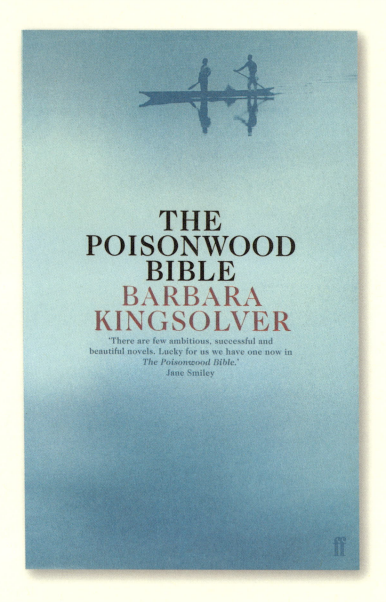

Barbara Kingsolver was first published by Faber in 1993. *The Poisonwood Bible*, the saga of an American missionary family in the Belgian Congo, published in 1999, was a phenomenal success, both critically and commercially, and was shortlisted for the Orange Prize.

JULY 2009

13 Monday BATTLE OF THE BOYNE HOLIDAY (IRL)

14 Tuesday

15 Wednesday

16 Thursday

17 Friday

18 Saturday   **19** Sunday

Seamus Heaney

Widgeon

for Paul Muldoon

It had been badly shot.
While he was plucking it
he found, he says, the voice box —

like a flute stop
in the broken windpipe —

and blew upon it
unexpectedly
his own small widgeon cries.

JULY 2009

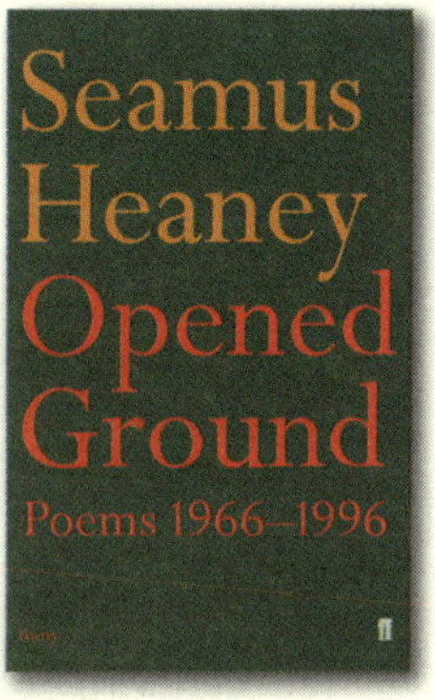

20 Monday

21 Tuesday

22 Wednesday

23 Thursday

24 Friday

25 Saturday

26 Sunday

Faber fiction: John Lanchester and Andrew O'Hagan

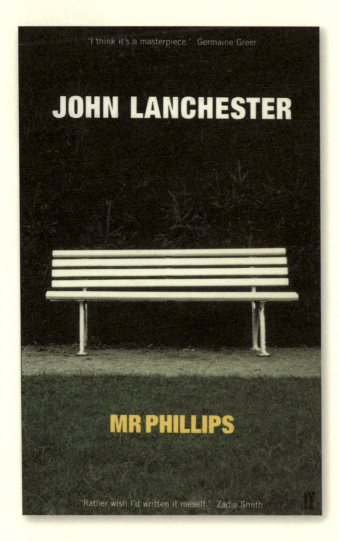

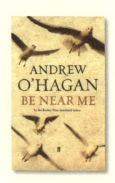

A new generation of British novelists rose to prominence in the nineties, including Andrew O'Hagan and John Lanchester. *Our Fathers*, O'Hagan's debut novel, was shortlisted for the 1999 Booker Prize. In 2000, John Lanchester came to Faber with his second novel, *Mr Phillips* – a funny and affecting study of redundancy and middle age. Both authors rapidly became mainstays of the Faber list. O'Hagan's poignant story of a lonely priest's fall from grace, *Be Near Me*, appeared in 2006, while Lanchester's memoir *Family Romance* was published in 2007.

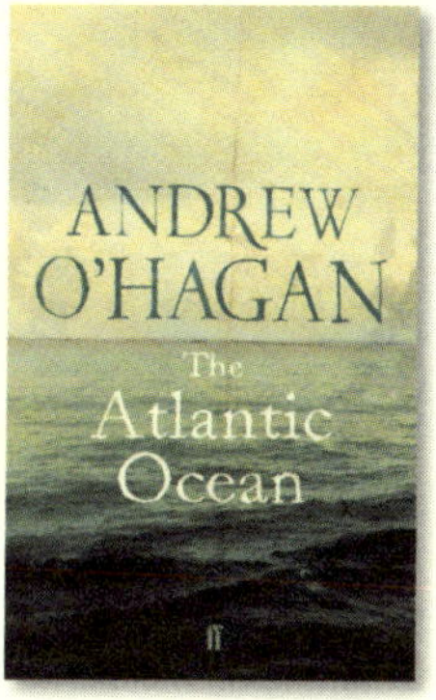

JULY/AUGUST 2009

27 Monday

28 Tuesday

29 Wednesday

30 Thursday

31 Friday

1 Saturday

2 Sunday

The Faber Book of . . .

In the nineties, some of Faber's new books would have seemed inconceivable to its first directors, but the company's sometimes quirky anthologies look back to the eccentric compilations of former days. Roy Porter's *Faber Book of Madness* was followed by Faber Books of *London*, *Espionage*, *Theatre* and *Movie Verse*. *The Faber Book of Reportage* and *The Faber Book of Science*, both edited by John Carey, have been the most successful and long lived.

AUGUST 2009

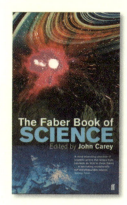

3 Monday BANK HOLIDAY (SCT, IRL, AU: NSW)

4 Tuesday

5 Wednesday

6 Thursday

7 Friday

8 Saturday   **9** Sunday WOMEN'S DAY (ZA)

Faber comic novels

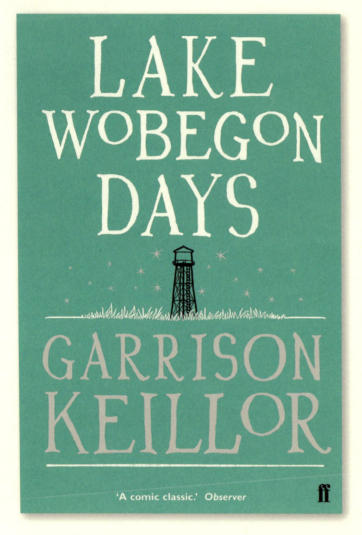
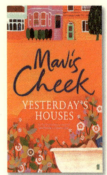

There is a long tradition of the comic novel at Faber, with distinguished British contributions from the likes of Joe Connolly and Nigel Williams, Andrew Martin, James Hamilton-Paterson and Mavis Cheek. From America comes Garrison Keillor and his stories of a Midwestern town 'where all the women are strong, all the men are good-looking, and all the children are above average'. Faber published *Lake Wobegon Days*, the first Wobegon novel, in 1986.

AUGUST 2009

10 Monday   PUBLIC HOLIDAY (ZA)

11 Tuesday

12 Wednesday

13 Thursday

14 Friday

15 Saturday   **16** Sunday

Wendy Cope

Flowers

Some men never think of it.
You did. You'd come along
And say you'd nearly brought me flowers
But something had gone wrong.

The shop was closed. Or you had doubts –
The sort that minds like ours
Dream up incessantly. You thought
I might not want your flowers.

It made me smile and hug you then.
Now I can only smile.
But, look, the flowers you nearly brought
Have lasted all this while.

AUGUST 2009

17 Monday

Wendy
Cope
Serious
Concerns

18 Tuesday

19 Wednesday

20 Thursday

21 Friday

22 Saturday   **23** Sunday

'No one ever told me that grief felt so like fear.'

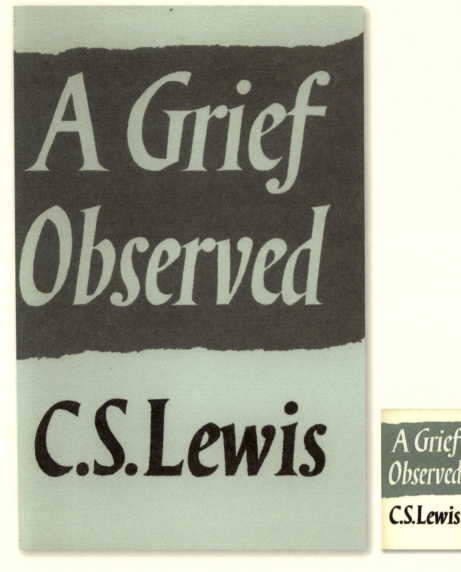

Widely regarded as one of the most comforting books written on the subject of loss, *A Grief Observed* was first published in 1961 under the pseudonym N. W. Clerk. Despite the secrecy, Lewis was quickly recognised by readers and critics as the author. The 1964 edition was the first to be published under the author's real name.

AUGUST 2009

24 Monday

25 Tuesday

26 Wednesday

27 Thursday

28 Friday

29 Saturday   **30** Sunday

'riverrun, past Eve and Adam's from swerve of shore to bend of bay . . .'

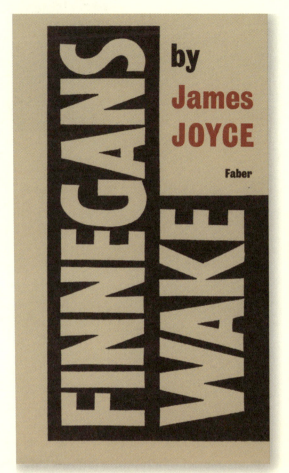
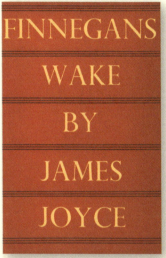

Eliot wrote to James Joyce in January 1934 to say that Faber 'were prepared to publish "Ulysses" as soon as publication proved feasible'. In August that year, Joyce, grumpy at the firm's tardiness, was dubbing it 'Feebler and Fumbler'. Eliot's caution about *Ulysses*, a work that was widely condemned as obscene, conquered his own admiration for it. The firm feared prosecution. Eventually, in 1936, John Lane brought out the Bodley Head edition of the novel, the first to be printed in Britain. Yet still Joyce, when he was not railing against publishers and printers in general, trusted to 'my friend T. S. Eliot' to shepherd his writing into print. Eliot had published a fragment of what was to become *Finnegans Wake* as early as July 1925, in the *Criterion*. In July 1931, he contracted with Joyce for Faber and Faber to publish the work. Faber was finally able to announce *Finnegans Wake*, by 'one of the very greatest of modern authors' in 1939.

AUGUST/SEPTEMBER 2009

31 Monday　LATE SUMMER (GB)

1 Tuesday

2 Wednesday

3 Thursday

4 Friday

5 Saturday　　　　　　　　**6** Sunday

Faber drama: Pinter and Ayckbourn

Harold Pinter, already at the height of his powers when he joined the Faber drama list in 1981 with *Family Voices*, was awarded the Nobel Prize for Literature in 2005. Alan Ayckbourn arrived at Faber in 1986, with two plays, *A Chorus of Disapproval* and *Woman in Mind*.

SEPTEMBER 2009

7 Monday LABOUR DAY (CA)

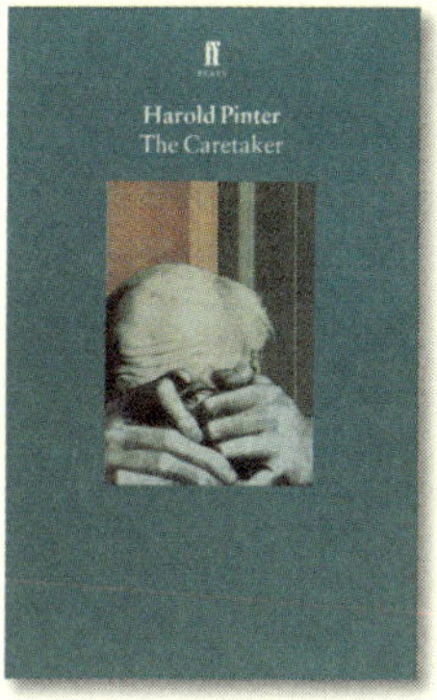

8 Tuesday

9 Wednesday

10 Thursday

11 Friday

12 Saturday   **13** Sunday

'It's hot as hell in Martirio . . .'

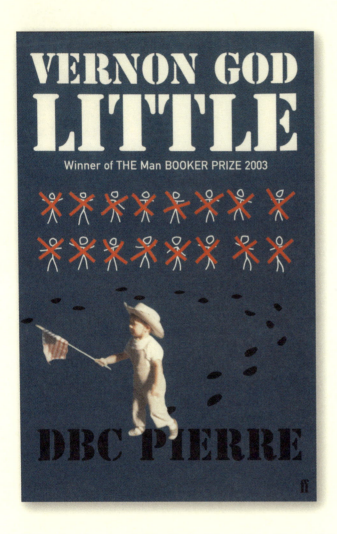

Faber authors have won the Man Booker Prize six times. The very first prize was awarded to P. H. Newby in 1969 for *Something to Answer For*. Most recently, Australian-born DBC Pierre's astonishing coup was to win the 2003 prize with his debut novel. The tragicomic and unforgettable *Vernon God Little* follows its charismatic title character – fifteen-year-old Vernon – in the aftermath of a shooting at a Texan school. His second novel was the equally outrageous and experimental *Ludmila's Broken English*, a novel about recently separated conjoined twins and their pursuit of a Russian mail-order bride.

SEPTEMBER 2009

14 Monday

15 Tuesday

16 Wednesday

17 Thursday

18 Friday

19 Saturday					**20** Sunday

Telegraph Wires

Take telegraph wires, a lonely moor,
And fit them together. The thing comes alive in your ear.

Towns whisper to towns over the heather.
But the wires cannot hide from the weather.

So oddly, so daintily made
It is picked up and played.

Such unearthly airs
The ear hears, and withers!

In the revolving ballroom of space,
Bowed over the moor, a bright face

Draws out of the telegraph wires the tones
That empty human bones.

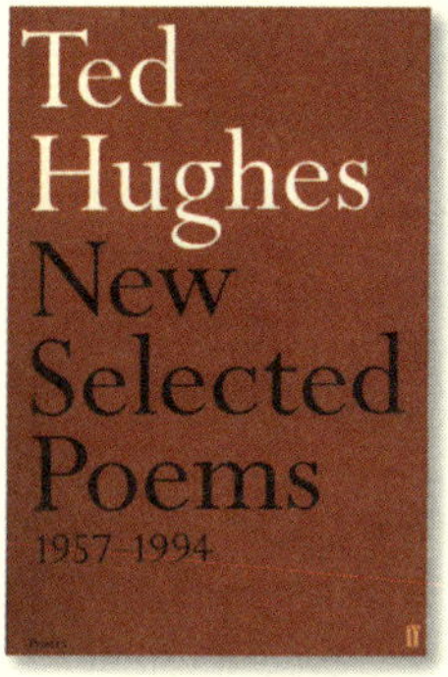

SEPTEMBER 2009

21 Monday

22 Tuesday

23 Wednesday

24 Thursday HERITAGE DAY (ZA)

25 Friday

26 Saturday

27 Sunday

'A splash of light from the late-afternoon sun lingered . . .'

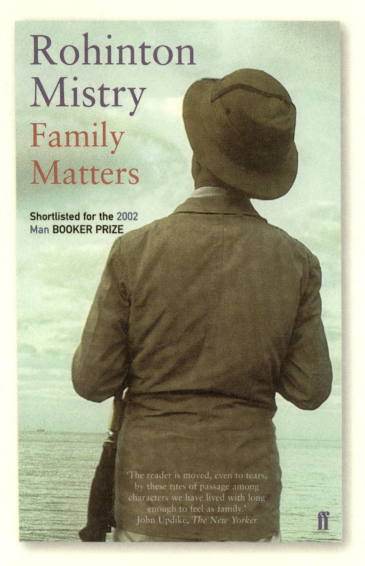

Born in Bombay in 1952, Rohinton Mistry moved to Canada in his early twenties. Over the course of three novels and a collection of stories, he has emerged as an author who can move and captivate readers around the world. The list of prizes Mistry has been awarded is remarkable, including the Commonwealth Writers' Prize (twice), the Canadian Governor General's Award and the Giller Prize. He has been shortlisted for the Booker Prize no less than three times.

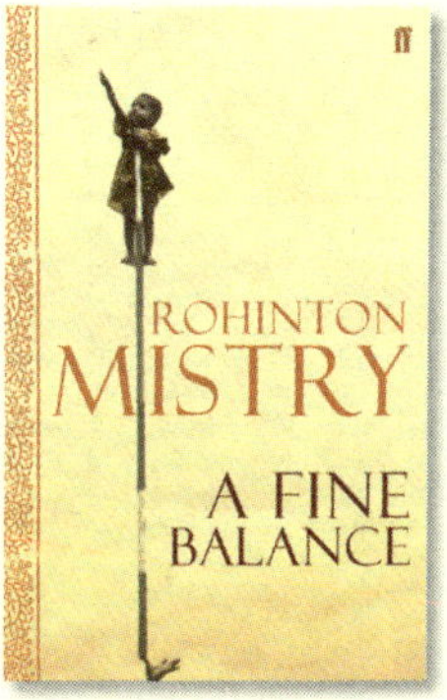

SEPTEMBER/OCTOBER 2009

28 Monday

29 Tuesday

30 Wednesday

1 Thursday

2 Friday

3 Saturday   **4** Sunday

'The soil in Leitrim is poor, in places no more than an inch deep.'

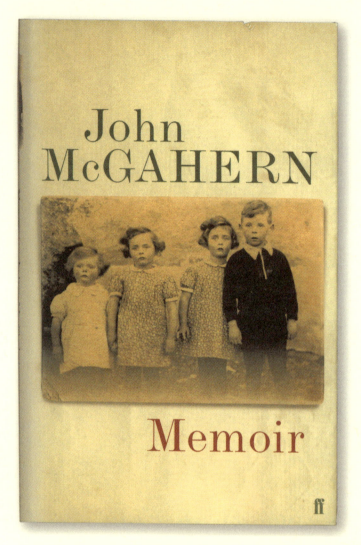

Memoir, published a year before McGahern's death in 2006, is regarded as his final magisterial achievement. His relationship with Faber began with his first novel, *The Barracks*, in 1963. *The Dark* (1965) was banned by the Irish State Censorship Board as 'indecent or obscene', 1990's *Amongst Women* brought a shortlisting for the Booker Prize. McGahern's late masterpiece, *That They May Face the Rising Sun*, included a thinly disguised portrait of his original publisher, Charles Monteith – brilliant, courteous, ungainly – as a partner in a small advertising company.

OCTOBER 2009

5 Monday LABOUR DAY (AU, NZ)

6 Tuesday

7 Wednesday

8 Thursday

9 Friday

10 Saturday   **11** Sunday

'Ann, Ann! / Come! Quick as you can!'

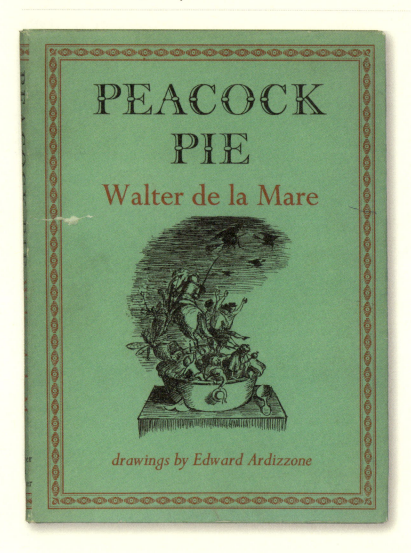

According to W. H. Auden, *Peacock Pie* is 'a revelation of the wonders of the English language, [and] de la Mare's poems for children are quite unrivalled'. Still in print from the 1940s, *Peacock Pie* is Walter de la Mare's most treasured collection. A 'book of rhymes', this marvellous anthology has been enjoyed by generations of children, and variously illustrated by W. Heath Robinson, C. Lovat Fraser, Jocelyn Crowe, F. R. Emett and Louise Brierley. In 1946, Faber published an edition with striking line drawings by Edward Ardizzone, which forms the basis for the current volume in the Faber Children's Classics series.

OCTOBER 2009

12 Monday   THANKSGIVING (CA)

13 Tuesday

14 Wednesday

15 Thursday

16 Friday

17 Saturday

18 Sunday

Philip Larkin

Days

What are days for?
Days are where we live.
They come, they wake us
Time and time over.
They are to be happy in:
Where can we live but days?

Ah, solving that question
Brings the priest and the doctor
In their long coats
Running over the fields.

OCTOBER 2009

19 Monday

20 Tuesday

21 Wednesday

22 Thursday

23 Friday

24 Saturday

25 Sunday   BRITISH SUMMER TIME ENDS

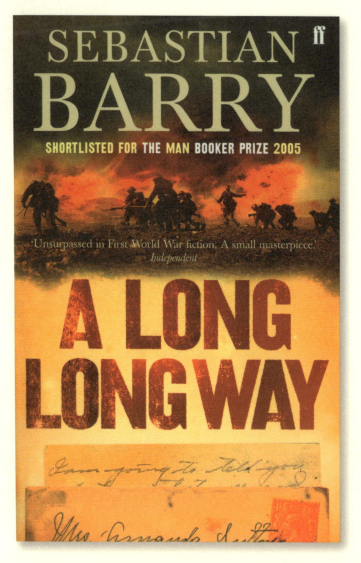

A number of playwrights have also written novels, but Michael Frayn and Sebastian Barry have achieved spectacular success in both arenas. Frayn's novels include *Headlong*, which was shortlisted for the 1999 Booker Prize, and *Spies*, which won the 2002 Whitbread Novel Award. Barry's *A Long, Long Way* was shortlisted for the 2005 Booker Prize and the Dublin International IMPAC Prize, while his most recent novel, *The Secret Scripture*, was published to huge acclaim in 2008.

OCTOBER/NOVEMBER 2009

26 Monday   LABOUR DAY (NZ), OCTOBER BANK HOLIDAY (IRL)

27 Tuesday

28 Wednesday

29 Thursday

30 Friday

31 Saturday   HALLOWEEN   **1** Sunday

'Compost-making may be either just a troublesome job or an absorbing occupation.'

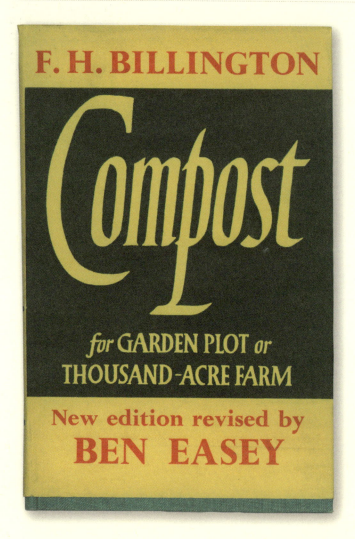

Specialist books began appearing in the 1940s as a response to the rigours of wartime civilian life. Titles on 'Farming, Gardening and the Open Air', flourished under Richard de la Mare, who was a pioneer of the organic movement and the Soil Association. The Faber list appropriately included the once renowned *Harnessing the Earthworm*. There were also books on bee-keeping, fishing and ornithology. And there were a significant number of practical guides to what we might call 'self-sufficiency': *A Fruitgrower's Diary* and *Common-Sense Compost Making*, *Early Potatoes* and the impressively detailed *Pig Curing and Cooking*.

NOVEMBER 2009

2 Monday

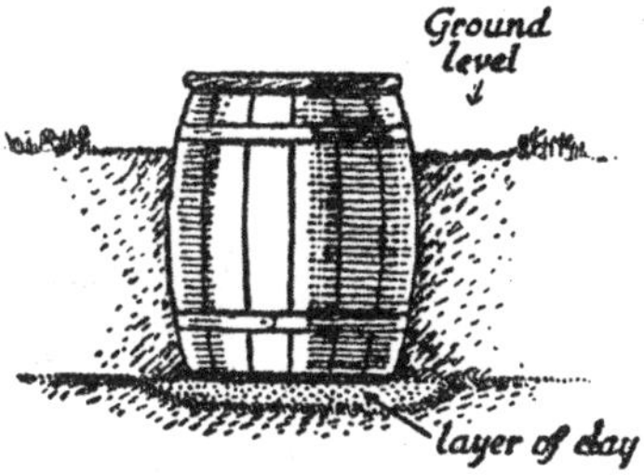

3 Tuesday

4 Wednesday

5 Thursday GUY FAWKES NIGHT

6 Friday

7 Saturday

8 Sunday REMEMBRANCE SUNDAY

'If there was a bishop, my mother would have him to tea.'

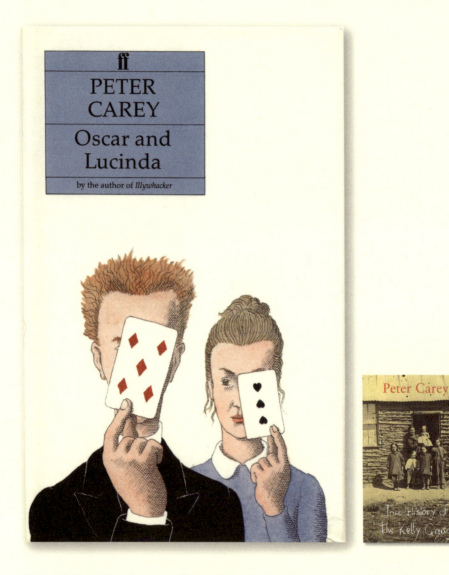

Robert McCrum's first discovery as Fiction Editor in the early 1980s was Peter Carey. Since joining Faber, Carey has published nine highly acclaimed novels and has won the Booker Prize twice. In 2008 Faber published *His Illegal Self*.

NOVEMBER 2009

9 Monday

10 Tuesday

11 Wednesday

12 Thursday

13 Friday

14 Saturday   **15** Sunday

T. S. Eliot

Preludes

I

The winter evening settles down
With smell of steaks in passageways.
Six o'clock.
The burnt-out ends of smoky days.
And now a gusty shower wraps
The grimy scraps
Of withered leaves about your feet
And newspapers from vacant lots;
The showers beat
On broken blinds and chimney-pots,
And at the corner of the street
A lonely cab-horse steams and stamps.

And then the lighting of the lamps.

NOVEMBER 2009

16 Monday

17 Tuesday

18 Wednesday

19 Thursday

20 Friday

21 Saturday	22 Sunday

Faber music books

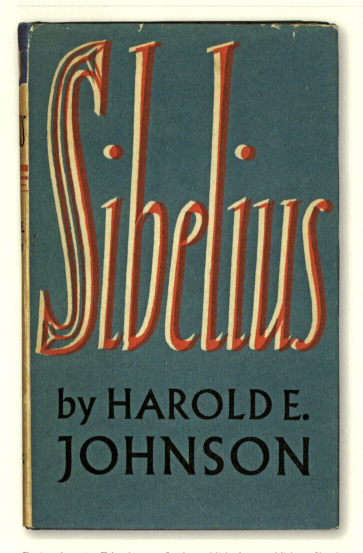

During the 1960s Faber became firmly established as a publisher of books on music, and remains in the forefront of music-book publishing. Established classics include the Stravinsky–Craft *Conversations*, Charles Rosen's *The Classical Style*, Elizabeth Wilson's *Shostakovich: A Life Remembered* and a dazzling collection of composers' letters: Bartók, Berg, Berlioz, Britten, Janáček, Schoenberg, Stravinsky, Shostakovich, Toscanini, Walton and Mozart. Embracing a wide readership, the list today includes *Why Beethoven Threw the Stew*, the first of two bestselling books for children by Steven Isserlis, and many titles on popular culture, notably *Rip it Up and Start Again* by Simon Reynolds.

NOVEMBER 2009

23 Monday

24 Tuesday

25 Wednesday

26 Thursday

27 Friday

28 Saturday

29 Sunday

'A meditation for radio.'

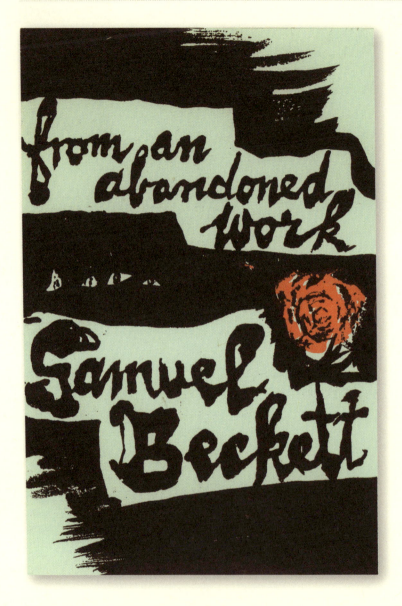

Samuel Beckett arrived at Faber with *Waiting for Godot* in 1956 and went on to publish *All That Fall* the next year. *Endgame* followed in 1958 and a volume containing *Krapp's Last Tape* and *Embers* in 1959. In 2008 it was announced that Beckett's novels and other writing would join his drama at Faber. Reissues of his works will begin this year.

NOVEMBER/DECEMBER 2009

30 Monday ST ANDREW'S DAY (SCT)

1 Tuesday

2 Wednesday

3 Thursday

4 Friday

5 Saturday   6 Sunday

'The boy with fair hair lowered himself down the last few feet of rock...'

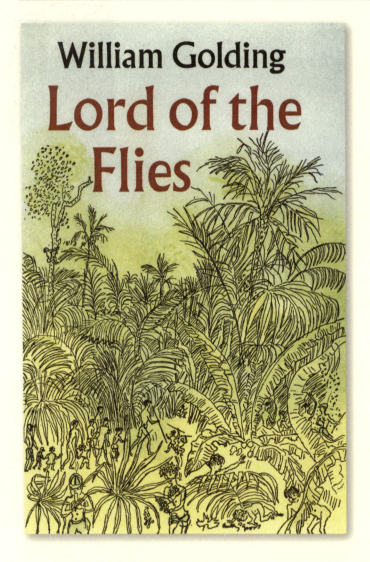

In 1954, William Golding's *Lord of the Flies* found an appreciative reader at Faber after it had been rejected by numerous other publishers. It was spotted by Charles Monteith, who discovered the typescript in the slush pile – a collection of unsolicited manuscripts. The text he unearthed was dog-eared from the number of hands through which it had passed and was called *Strangers from Within*. Monteith contacted Golding and persuaded him to make significant cuts and revisions, and to change the title to *Lord of the Flies*.

DECEMBER 2009

7 Monday

8 Tuesday

9 Wednesday

10 Thursday

11 Friday

12 Saturday   **13** Sunday

W. H. Auden

XXIX Gare du Midi

A nondescript express in from the South,
Crowds round the ticket barrier, a face
To welcome which the mayor has not contrived
Bugles or braid: something about the mouth
Distracts the stray look with alarm and pity.
Snow is falling. Clutching a little case,
He walks out briskly to infect a city
Whose terrible future may have just arrived.

DECEMBER 2009

14 Monday

15 Tuesday

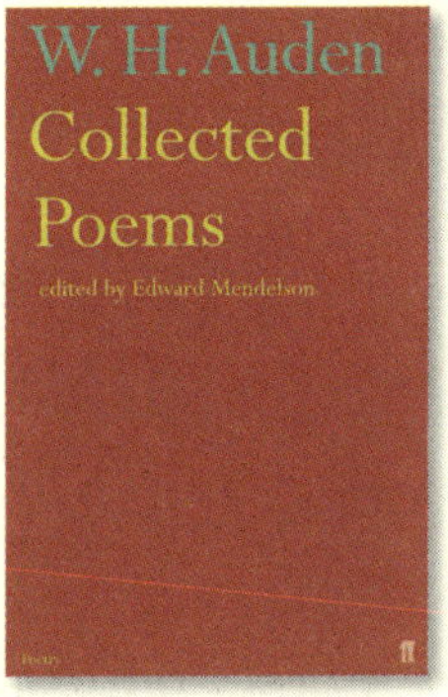

16 Wednesday   DAY OF RECONCILIATION (ZA)

17 Thursday

18 Friday

19 Saturday   **20** Sunday

Christmas 1946

Faber has a tradition of commissioning a Christmas card from one of the illustrators closely associated with the company. This card by Barnett Freedman was the second to be produced for the staff to send to customers and friends. His design for Christmas 1945 read 'With every good wish for the first Christmas and New Year of Peace', and it is clear from the iconography and the message (peace on earth) on the 1946 design that this sentiment was still very keenly felt.

DECEMBER 2009

21 Monday

22 Tuesday

23 Wednesday

24 Thursday

25 Friday   CHRISTMAS DAY (GB, IRL, CA, AU, NZ)

26 Saturday   BOXING DAY,
DAY OF GOODWILL (ZA)

27 Sunday

'So the Venetians became islanders and islanders they remain...'

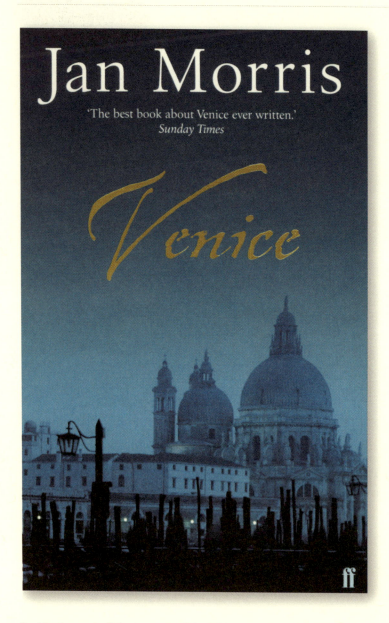

Jan Morris came to Faber in 1956, and the publication of her sixth book, *Venice*, in 1960, established her as a major author on the list. *Venice* is an acknowledged classic of twentieth-century travel writing, which continues to sell thousands of copies every year.

DECEMBER 2009 / JANUARY 2010

28 Monday   DECEMBER HOLIDAY (GB, IRL, CA, AU)

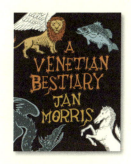

29 Tuesday

30 Wednesday

31 Thursday

1 Friday

2 Saturday

3 Sunday

A Short History of Faber and Faber

1925 Geoffrey Faber acquires an interest in The Scientific Press and renames the firm Faber and Gwyer ¶ The poet/bank clerk T. S. Eliot is recruited. 'What will impress my directors favourably is the sense that in you we have found a man who combines literary gifts with business instincts.' – Geoffrey Faber to T. S. Eliot ¶

1929 The birth of the Faber and Faber imprint. 'Our first directors' meeting of F & F Ltd. I feel in my bones that the thing is going to work out.' – Geoffrey Faber's diary ¶ Siegfried Sassoon's *Memoirs of a Fox-Hunting Man* provides the earliest bestseller ¶

1930 Publication of T. S. Eliot's first title for Faber, *Ash Wednesday*. 'Wavering between the profit and the loss / In this brief transit where dreams cross.' ¶ The young W. H. Auden becomes a Faber author. 'If this really is only the beginning, we have perhaps a master to look forward to.' – Naomi Mitchison ¶

1931 Alison Uttley comes to Faber with *The Country Child* ¶

1932 Stephen Spender becomes a Faber poet ¶

1935 The American poet Marianne Moore publishes with Faber. 'Miss Moore's poems form part of a small body of durable poetry written in our time.'– T. S. Eliot ¶ Louis MacNeice becomes a Faber poet. 'The most original Irish poet of his generation.'– Faber catalogue, 1935 ¶

1936 The hugely influential *Faber Book of Modern Verse* (edited by Michael Roberts) published ¶ Djuna Barnes comes to Faber with *Nightwood* ¶

1937 Neil M. Gunn wins the James Tait Black Memorial Prize with *Highland River* ¶

1939 Eliot publishes *Old Possum's Book of Practical Cats* ¶ James Joyce's *Finnegans Wake* published ¶ Faber takes over the Shell Guides to English Counties ¶

1940 Despite the war, Faber publishes 180 titles in 1940 ¶

1944 The Faber Gallery is launched to strengthen Faber's arts list. 'The price is 6s. and for this you get good paper, elegant typography, a scholarly text and, most importantly, excellent colour in the reproductions.' – *Time and Tide* ¶ Walter de la Mare's *Peacock Pie* published with illustrations by Edward Ardizzone ¶ Philip Larkin's first novel, *A Girl in Winter*, published. 'A young man with an exceptionally clear sense of what, as a writer, he means to do.' – *Times Literary Supplement* ¶

1948 T. S. Eliot wins the Nobel Prize in Literature ¶

1949 Ezra Pound's *Pisan Cantos* published. 'The most incomprehensible passages are often more stimulating than much comprehensibility which passes for poetry today.' *Times Literary Supplement* ¶

1950 Robert Lowell joins the Faber poets ¶

1953 Gerald Durrell comes to Faber with his first book, *The Overloaded Ark* ¶

1954 William Golding's *Lord of the Flies* published. 'Beautifully written, tragic and provocative.' – E. M. Forster ¶

1957 Jean Genet's *The Maids* published ¶ Ted Hughes comes to Faber with *The Hawk in the Rain* ¶ Lawrence Durrell's *Justine* published. 'Mr Durrell is more than a novelist; he is a writer.' – Cyril Connolly ¶

1958 Faber publishes its first paperbacks ¶ Faber director David Bland publishes his influential *History of Book Illustration* ¶

1960 Richard de la Mare becomes Chairman of Faber ¶ Saint-John Perse wins the Nobel Prize in Literature ¶

1961 Geoffrey Faber dies ¶ Ted Hughes's first book of children's poems, *Meet My Folks*, published ¶

1962 P. D. James comes to Faber with *Cover Her Face* ¶

1963 Sylvia Plath's novel *The Bell Jar* published by Faber in the year of her death ¶

1964 Larkin's *The Whitsun Weddings* published ¶

1965 T. S. Eliot dies ¶ Faber Music launched ¶ Sylvia Plath's posthumous collection *Ariel* published. 'Her extraordinary achievement, poised as she was between her volatile emotional state and the edge of the precipice.' – Frieda Hughes ¶

1966 Seamus Heaney comes to Faber with *Death of a Naturalist* ¶

1967 Faber issued the first ever children's books in paper covers ¶ Tom Stoppard's *Rosencrantz and Guildenstern Are Dead* published ¶ Peter Nichols's *A Day in the Death of Joe Egg* published ¶

1968 Ted Hughes's *The Iron Man* published ¶

1969 The first Booker Prize awarded to P. H. Newby's *Something to Answer For* ¶ Samuel Beckett wins the Nobel Prize in Literature ¶

1970 Peter du Sautoy becomes Chairman ¶ David Hare comes to Faber with his first play, *Slag*. 'A grasp of stunning dialogue, assured wit and theatrical virtuosity astonishing from one so young.' – Milton Shulman ¶

1971 Thomas Kilroy's *The Big Chapel* is short-listed for the Booker Prize ¶

1972 Matthew Evans becomes Managing Director ¶

1973 Paul Muldoon comes to Faber with his first collection, *New Weather* ¶ Ruth Spalding's biography of Bulstrode Whitelock, *The Improbable Puritan*, wins the Whitbread Prize for a First Book ¶

1975 Berthold Wolpe retires, having placed Faber design at the forefront of British publishing ¶

1977 Gene Kemp's *The Turbulent Term of Tyke Tiler* published, the first children's novel ever set in a comprehensive school ¶ Tom Paulin comes to Faber with his first collection, *A State of Justice* ¶ Historian Christopher Hill's major work *Milton and the English Revolution* published ¶

1978 Maurice Gee's *Plumb* wins the James Tait Black Memorial Prize ¶

1980 Csezlaw Milosz wins the Nobel Prize in Literature ¶ Golding's *Rites of Passage* wins the Booker Prize. 'Simply the best living writer of the short novel in the English language.' – *The Times* ¶

1981 Peter Carey's first novel, *Bliss*, published. '[A] quirky, irresistible first novel.' – *Time Out* ¶ Pentagram give a makeover to the Faber house style ¶ *Cats*, the musical based on *Old Possum*, opens in London ¶

1982 Kazuo Ishiguro comes to Faber with *A Pale View of Hills*. 'One of the outstanding fictional debuts of recent years.' – *Observer* ¶ Milan Kundera's *Book of Laughter and Forgetting* published ¶ Lawrence Durrell's *Constance or Solitary Practices* is shortlisted for the Booker Prize ¶

1983 Mario Vargas Llosa's *Aunt Julia and the Scriptwriter* published. 'As full of fizz as a pack of sherbert.' – *Sunday Times* ¶ Faber screenplays launched ¶ William Golding wins the Nobel Prize in Literature ¶

1984 *Rich*, a collection by Faber's own poetry editor, Craig Raine, is published. 'Puts us in touch with life as unexpectedly and joyfully as early Pasternak.' – John Bayley ¶

1985 Douglas Dunn's *Elegies* is the Whitbread Book of the Year ¶ Peter Carey's *Illywhacker* is shortlisted for the Booker Prize ¶

1986   Faber's second consecutive Whitbread Book of the Year with Kazuo Ishiguro's *An Artist of the Floating World*, which is also shortlisted for the Booker Prize ¶ Garrison Keillor comes to Faber with *Lake Wobegone Days*. 'A cast of characters to rival Mark Twain.' – *Daily Mail* ¶ Vikram Seth's *The Golden Gate* published. ¶

1987   Paul Auster comes to Faber with *The New York Trilogy*. 'Written with an acid sharpness that leaves an indelible dent on the mind.' – *Sunday Telegraph* ¶ Seamus Heaney's *The Haw Lantern* wins the Whitbread Prize for Poetry ¶

1988   Peter Carey's *Oscar and Lucinda* wins the Booker Prize ¶

1989   Kazuo Ishiguro's *The Remains of the Day* wins the Booker Prize ¶

1990   Faber moves into new fields with *The Faber Companion to Twentieth-Century Popular Music* ¶ John McGahern's *Amongst Women* is shortlisted for the Booker Prize. 'McGahern brings us that tonic gift of the best fiction, the sense of truth . . . a sight that cleanses us even as it saddens and frightens.' – John Updike ¶ Two Whitbread Prizes for Faber authors, with Hanif Kureishi's *The Buddha of Suburbia* and Ann Thwaite's biography of A. A. Milne ¶

1991   Rohinton Mistry comes to Faber with *Such a Long Journey* which is shortlisted for the Booker Prize. 'Undoubtedly one of the best novels from India in recent years.' – *Spectator* ¶

1992   Derek Walcott wins the Nobel Prize in Literature ¶

1993   Andrew Motion wins the Whitbread Prize for Biography for his book on *Philip Larkin* ¶ Barbara Kingsolver comes to Faber with *Pigs in Heaven* ¶

1994   The screenplay of *Pulp Fiction* published. It goes on to sell a quarter of a million copies ¶

Alan Bennett's *Writing Home* published. It goes on to sell 700,000 copies ¶ Seamus Heaney wins the Nobel Prize in Literature ¶

1995   Wislawa Szymborska wins the Nobel Prize in Literature ¶ Seamus Heaney's *The Spirit Level* wins the Whitbread Prize for Poetry. 'Touched by a sense of wonder.' – Blake Morrison ¶

1996   Mavis Cheek comes to Faber with her novel *Sleeping Beauties* ¶ Ted Hughes's *Tales from Ovid* is the Whitbread Book of the Year. 'A breathtaking book.' – John Carey ¶ Rohinton Mistry's *A Fine Balance* is shortlisted for the Booker Prize ¶ Jane Rogers's *Promised Lands* is shortlisted for the Orange Prize for Fiction ¶

1997   Don Paterson wins the T. S. Eliot Prize for *God's Gift to Women* ¶ Deirdre Madden's *One by One in the Darkness* is shortlisted for the Orange Prize for Fiction ¶

1998   Ted Hughes wins the Whitbread Book of the Year for the second time running with *The Birthday Letters*, which also wins the T. S. Eliot Prize. 'Language like lava, its molten turmoils hardening into jagged shapes.' – John Carey ¶

1999   Günter Grass wins the Nobel Prize in Literature ¶ Michael Frayn's *Headlong* and also Andrew O'Hagan's *Our Fathers* are both shortlisted for the Booker Prize ¶ Seamus Heaney's *Beowulf* wins the Whitbread Book of the Year Award. '[Heaney is the] one living poet who can rightly claim to be Beowulf's heir.' – *New York Times* ¶ Hugo Williams wins the T. S. Eliot Prize for his collection *Billy's Rain* ¶ *The Poisonwood Bible* by Barbara Kingsolver is shortlisted for the Orange Prize for Fiction ¶

2000   Peter Carey wins the Booker Prize for a second time with *True History of the Kelly Gang* ¶ Kazuo Ishiguro's *When We Were Orphans* is shortlisted for the Booker Prize ¶

2001 *Blue Tango* by Eoin McNamee longlisted for the Booker Prize ¶ *Horse Heaven* by Jane Smiley is shortlisted for the Orange prize for Fiction ¶ Virginia Euwer Wolff shortlisted for the Carnegie Medal in 2001 for *Make Lemonade* ¶

2002 Jenny Uglow's *The Lunar Men* wins the James Tait Black Memorial Prize for Biography. 'An exhilarating book, full of wonder.' – Peter Ackroyd ¶ Rohinton Mistry's *Family Matters* is shortlisted for the Booker Prize ¶ Michael Frayn's *Spies* is the Whitbread Novel of the Year and longlisted for the Booker Prize. 'The most philosophical comic writer – the most comic philosophical writer.' – *Daily Mail* ¶ Alice Oswald wins the T. S. Eliot Prize for *Dart* ¶

2003 DBC Pierre's first novel, *Vernon God Little*, wins the Booker Prize. 'Original, engaging and fantastically well structured.' – *Daily Telegraph* ¶ Andrew O'Hagan's *Personality* wins the James Tait Black Memorial Prize ¶ Orhan Pamuk's *My Name Is Red* wins the IMPAC Prize ¶ G. P. Taylor's Shadowmancer published. 'The biggest event in children's fiction since Harry Potter.' – *The Times* ¶

2004 David Peace's *GB84* wins the James Tait Black Memorial Prize. 'If Northern Noir is the crime fashion at the moment, Peace is its most brilliant designer.' – *The Times* ¶ Nadeem Aslam's *Maps for Lost Lovers* is longlisted for the Booker Prize ¶ Sarah Hall's *The Electric Michelangelo* is shortlisted for the Booker Prize ¶

2005 Rachel Cusk's *In the Fold* is longlisted for the Booker Prize ¶ Sebastian Barry's *A Long, Long Way* and Kazuo Ishiguro's *Never Let Me Go* are both shortlisted for the Booker Prize ¶ Harold Pinter wins the Nobel Prize for Literature ¶ David Harsent wins the Forward Prize for *Legion* ¶

2006 Christopher Logue wins the Whitbread Prize for Poetry for *Cold Calls* ¶ Daren King's *Mouse Noses on Toast* wins the Nestlé Children's Book Prize Gold Medal ¶ Peter Carey's *Theft: A Love Story* and Andrew O'Hagan's *Be Near Me* are both longlisted for the Booker Prize ¶ Orhan Pamuk wins the Nobel Prize for Literature ¶ Geoffrey Faber Memorial Prize is awarded to Alice Oswald for *Woods etc.* ¶ Seamus Heaney wins the T. S. Eliot Prize for *District and Circle* ¶ Alan Bennett is named Author of the Year at the British Book Awards ¶ Jane Smiley wins the PEN Lifetime Achievement Award ¶ John McGahern wins the South Bank Show Award for Literature ¶ Faber and Faber is named Publisher of the Year at the British Book Awards ¶ James Shapiro wins the BBC4 Samuel Johnson Prize for *1599: A Year in the Life of William Shakespeare* ¶ John Lloyd and John Mitchinson's hugely successful *Book of General Ignorance* published, a mere twenty-one years after *Spitting Image*, Lloyd's previous book with Faber ¶

2007 Michael Dibdin dies, shortly before the publication of *End Games* ¶ *The Observations* by Jane Harris and *Arlington Park* by Rachel Cusk are shortlisted for the Orange Prize for Fiction ¶ Sarah Hall's *Carhullan Army* wins the John Llewellyn Rhys Prize ¶ Tony Harrison is awarded the Wilfred Owen Award for Poetry ¶ Tom Stoppard's *Rock 'n' Roll* wins the Critics' Circle Award 2007 for Best New Play and the *Evening Standard* Award for Best New Play ¶ Daljit Nagra's *Look We Have Coming to Dover!* wins the Forward Prize for Best First Collection ¶

2008 David Peace is shortlisted for the Reader's Digest Author of the Year at the British Book Awards ¶ Betty G. Birney's *Adventure According to Humphrey* is chosen for World Book Day ¶ Daljit Nagra wins the South Bank Show/Arts Council Decibel Award ¶ *The Carhullan Army* by Sarah Hall and *The H-Bomb Girl* by Stephen Baxter are both shortlisted for the Arthur C. Clarke Award ¶ Junot Diaz's *The Brief Wondrous Life of Oscar Wao* wins the Pulitzer Prize ¶ Joanna Kavenna wins the Orange Broadband Award for New Writers for *Inglorious* ¶

2009 . . .

The Poets

Simon Armitage was born in West Yorkshire in 1963. In 1992 he was winner of one of the first Forward Prizes, and a year later was the *Sunday Times* Young Writer of the Year. He works as a freelance writer, broadcaster and playwright, and has written extensively for radio and television. Previous titles include *Kid*, *Book of Matches*, *The Dead Sea Poems*, *CloudCuckooLand*, *Killing Time*, *The Universal Home Doctor*, *Homer's Odyssey* and *Tyrannosaurus Rex versus The Corduroy Kid*.

W. H. Auden was born in York in 1907, and brought up in Birmingham. He went to Christ Church College, Oxford, where Stephen Spender privately printed a booklet of his poems. After university he lived for a time in Berlin, before returning to England to teach. His first book, *Poems*, was published by T. S. Eliot at Faber in 1930. Other volumes of poems and plays followed throughout the 1930s. He went to Spain during the civil war, to Iceland (with Louis MacNeice) and later travelled to China. In 1939 he and Christopher Isherwood left for America, where Auden spent the next fifteen years lecturing, reviewing, writing poetry and opera librettos and editing anthologies. He became an American citizen in 1946, and was awarded the Pulitzer Prize in 1948. In 1956 he was elected Professor of Poetry at Oxford, and a year later went to live in Kirchstetten in Austria, after spending several summers on Ischia. He died in Vienna in 1973.

Wendy Cope was born in Erith, Kent, in 1945. After university she worked for fifteen years as a primary-school teacher in London. Her first collection of poems, *Making Cocoa for Kingsley Amis*, was published in 1986. In 1987 she received a Cholmondeley Award for Poetry and in 1995 the American Academy of Arts and Letters Michael Braude Award for Light Verse.

T. S. Eliot was born in St Louis, Missouri, in 1888. He was educated at Harvard, at the Sorbonne in Paris, and at Merton College, Oxford. He married Vivienne Haigh-Wood in 1915 and settled in England. He joined Lloyds Bank in the City of London in 1917 and in the same year published his first collection, *Prufrock and Other Observations*. In 1919, *Poems* was hand-printed by Leonard and

Virginia Woolf. His first collection of essays, *The Sacred Wood*, appeared in 1920. *The Waste Land* was published in 1922. It was included in the first issue of his journal the *Criterion*, which he founded and edited. His *Poems 1909–1925* was one of the original titles published by Faber and Faber and the basis of his standard *Collected Poems 1909-1962*. *Ash Wednesday* was published at Easter in 1930. His masterpiece *Four Quartets* began with 'Burnt Norton' in 1936, continued with 'East Coker' in 1940, 'The Dry Salvages' in 1941 and 'Little Gidding' in 1942. The separate poems were gathered together as one work in 1943. Eliot's writing for the theatre began with the satirical 'Sweeney Agonistes' fragments. In 1934 he wrote 'The Rock', the choruses from which are in *Collected Poems*. In 1942 he was commissioned by the Canterbury Festival to write *Murder in the Cathedral*. *The Family Reunion* followed in 1939, when he also published *Old Possum's Book of Practical Cats*. He wrote three more plays: *The Cocktail Party*, *The Confidential Clerk* and *The Elder Statesman*. Eliot's literary criticism is represented in *Selected Essays 1917–1932*. There are a number of other volumes of lectures and essays, including *The Use of Poetry and the Use of Criticism*, *For Lancelot Andrewes*, *On Poetry and Poets*, and two works of social criticism: *The Idea of a Christian Society* and *Notes towards the Definition of Culture*. Eliot was appointed to the Order of Merit in January 1948 and in the autumn was awarded the Nobel Prize for Literature. He married for the second time in 1957, to Valerie Fletcher. He died in January 1965. After his death his widow edited the long-lost original manuscript of the *The Waste Land* and a volume of his letters. She also commissioned a volume of his early poems, *Inventions of a March Hare*, and his Clark and Turnbull lectures, *The Varieties of Metaphysical Poetry*. He died in 1965.

Seamus Heaney was born in County Derry in Northern Ireland in 1939. *Death of a Naturalist*, his first collection, appeared in 1966, and since then he has published poetry, criticism and translations which have established him as one of the leading poets of his generation. In 1995 he was awarded the Nobel Prize for Literature. In 2007 his twelfth collection, *District and Circle*, was awarded the T. S. Eliot Prize.

Ted Hughes was born in Yorkshire in 1930. His first book, *The Hawk in the Rain*, was published in 1957 and was followed by many volumes of poetry and prose for adults and children. He received the Whitbread Book of the Year for two consecutive years for his last published collections of poetry, *Tales from Ovid* (1997) and *Birthday Letters* (1998). He was Poet Laureate from 1984 and in 1998 he was appointed to the Order of Merit. He died the same year.

Philip Larkin was born in Coventry in 1922 and was educated at King Henry VIII School, Coventry, and St John's College, Oxford. As well as his volumes of poems, which include *The Whitsun Weddings* and *High Windows*, he wrote the novels *Jill* and *A Girl in Winter* and two books of collected journalism, *All What Jazz: A Record Library* and *Required Writing: Miscellaneous Prose*. He worked as a librarian at the University of Hull from 1955 until his death in 1985. He was the recipient of numerous awards, including the Queen's Gold Medal for Poetry.

Marianne Moore was born near St Louis, Missouri, in 1887. She attended Bryn Mawr College and received her BA in 1909. Following graduation she worked first as a school teacher and in 1918 moved to New York. In 1921 she became an assistant at the New York Public Library. She began contributing poems to the *Dial*, a prestigious literary magazine, becoming its acting editor from 1925 to 1929. Moore received many prizes for her work, including the Bollingen Prize, the National Book Award and the Pulitzer Prize. She died in 1972.

Paul Muldoon was born in County Armagh in 1951. He read English at Queen's University, Belfast, and published his first collection of poems, *New Weather*, in 1973. He is the author of ten books of poetry, including *Mules* (1977), *Why Brownlee Left* (1980), *Quoof* (1983), *Meeting The British* (1987), *Madoc: A Mystery* (1990), *The Annals of Chile* (1994), *Hay* (1998), *Moy Sand and Gravel* (2002), for which he received the Pulitzer Prize for Poetry, and *Horse Latitudes* (2006). Since 1987 he has lived in the United States, where he is the Howard G. B. Clark Professor in the Humanities at Princeton University. From 1999 to 2004 he was the Professor of Poetry at Oxford University. A Fellow of the Royal Society of Literature, Paul Muldoon was given an American Academy of Arts and Letters Award in 1996. Other recent awards are the 1994 T. S. Eliot Prize, the 1997 *Irish Times* Poetry Prize, and the 2003 Griffin Prize.

Alice Oswald was born in 1966. She lives in Devon and is married with three children. Her first collection, *The Thing in the Gap-Stone Stile*, won the Forward Prize for Best First Collection in 1996. *Dart*, her second volume, won the T. S. Eliot Prize in 2002. Her third collection, *Woods etc.*, won the Geoffrey Faber Memorial Prize 2006.

Don Paterson was born in Dundee in 1963. He works as a musician and editor, and teaches at the University of St Andrews. He has written four collections of poetry: *Nil Nil*, *God's Gift to Women* (winner of both the T. S. Eliot Prize and the Geoffrey Faber Memorial Prize), *The Eyes* and *Landing Light* (winner of the Whitbread Prize for Poetry and the T. S. Eliot Prize). He lives in Kirriemuir, Angus.

Sylvia Plath was born in Boston, Massachusetts, in 1932, and studied at Smith College. In 1955 she went to Cambridge University on a Fulbright Scholarship, where she met and later married Ted Hughes. She published one collection of poems in her lifetime, *The Colossus* (1960), and a novel, *The Bell Jar* (1963). Her *Collected Poems*, which contains her poetry written from 1956 until her death in 1963, was published in 1981 and was awarded the Pulitzer Prize for Poetry.

Ezra Pound was born in Hailey, Idaho, in 1885. He came to Europe in 1898 and settled in London, where he was to meet Yeats, Eliot, Ford, Hulme and Gaudier-Brzeska. In 1920 he moved to Paris, and later to Rapallo. During the Second World War he broadcast over Rome Radio – for which, eventually, he was tried for treason in Washington. He was committed to a hospital for the insane, where he was held for thirteen years. He was released in 1958 and returned to Italy, dying in Venice in 1972. His main publications include *The Cantos (I-CXVII)*, *Collected Shorter Poems*, *Translations*, *The Confucian Odes*, *Literary Essays*, *Guide to Kulchur*, *Selected Prose* and *ABC of Reading*.

Picture Credits

Intro: George W. Adamson's illustration for *The Faber Book of Nursery Rhymes* reproduced by permission of the Adamson Estate, *Aunt Julia and the Scriptwriter* design by Andy Smith, *Vernon God Little* cover design by Pentagram ¶ December 29: William Nicholson's illustration and design for *Memoirs of a Fox-Hunting Man* reproduced by permission of Elizabeth Banks ¶ January 5: *Justine* design by Berthold Wolpe, author photo © Caroline Forbes ¶ January 12: *Philip Larkin: A Writer's Life* design by Pentagram, author photo reproduced by permission of the Larkin Estate, *Ways of Life* design by Faber, author photo by Johnny Ring, *In the Blood* design by Faber, author photograph courtesy of the author, *Selected Poems 1976–1997* cover design by Pentagram ¶ January 19: *Landing Light* design by Pentagram ¶ January 26: George W. Adamson's illustration for *The Iron Man* reproduced by permission of the Adamson Estate, *Iron Man* design by Andrew Davidson ¶ February 2: Benjamin Britten's letter reproduced by permission of the Trustees of the Britten-Pears Foundation, *Curlew River* design by Berthold Wolpe ¶ February 9: Charles Mozley's illustration and design for *Cover Her Face* reproduced by permission of the Mozley Trust, author photo by Alixe Buckerfield de la Roche ¶ February 16: *Ariel* design by Pentagram ¶ February 23: T. S. Eliot's illustration for *Old Possum's Book of Practical Cats* reproduced by permission of the Eliot Estate, new edition illustrated by Axel Scheffler ¶ March 2: *The Unbearable Lightness of Being* illustration reproduced by permission of Milan Kundera, author photo by Fridrik Rafusson ¶ March 9: *For the Union Dead, Whitsun Weddings*, and *Ariel* designs by Berthold Wolpe ¶ March 16: *Selected Poems 1908–1969* design by Pentagram ¶ March 23: *Projections 1* photo by The Douglas Brothers, *Projections 3* artwork by Ann Ross Paterson from a still, courtesy of the British Film Institute, *Projections 5* photo © Aardman Animations, *Projections 14* photo of Robert De Niro from *Casino* © 1995 Universal City Studios, Inc. ¶ March 30: *Tyrannosaurus Rex versus The Corduroy Kid* design by Pentagram ¶ April 6: Charles Monteith's memorandum © The Faber and Faber archive ¶ April 13: *The New York Trilogy* jacket illustration by Irene von Treskow, *Man in the Dark* design by Gavin Morris, photo © Reilika Landen/Archangel Images ¶ April 20: *Moy Sand and Gravel* design by Pentragram ¶ April 27: *The Bell Jar* design by Shirley Tucker, *Colossus* and *Crossing the Water* designs by Berthold Wolpe ¶ May 4: *Writing Home* author photo by Nigel Parry, design by Two Associates, *Untold Stories* author photo by Hugo Glendinning, *The Uncommon Reader* design by Peter Dyer ¶ 11 May: *The Buddha of Suburbia* illustration by Peter Blake, reproduced by permission of the artist, author photo by Sarah Lee ¶ May 18: *Woods etc.* design by Pentagram ¶ May 25 *My Name Is Red* design by Pentagram, *Other Colours* design by Gavin Morris at Faber, photo © Orhan Pamuk ¶ June 1: *Look Back in Anger* photo by Julie Hamilton, *Translations* design by Pentagram, photo by Larry Doherty ¶ June 8: *Remains of the Day* design by Pentagram, photo by Sam McConnell, author photo © Jane Brown ¶ June 15: *The Poems of Marianne Moore* photo by George Platt Lynes ¶ June 22: *The White Goddess* design by Berthold Wolpe ¶ June 29: illustration by David Roberts from *Final Curtain* by Phil Ardagh, *Awful End* design by Dave Crook with illustration by David Roberts ¶ July 6: *Slag* photo by John Haynes, *Les Liaisons Dangereuses* and *The Grace of Mary Traverse* designs by Pentagram ¶ July 13: *The Poisonwood Bible* image Congo River, Zaire © Mark Schlossman/Panos Pictures ¶ July 20: *Opened Ground* design by Pentagram ¶ July 27 *Mr Phillips* design by Pentagram, photo© Gunnar Smoliansky/Photonica, *Be Near Me* design by Darren Wall at Faber, photo © Stone/Getty Images and Roderick Field, *Atlantic Ocean* design by Faber, photo © Keith Goldstein/Photonica/Getty Images ¶ August 3: *The Faber Book of French Folk Songs* illustration by Edmée Arma, *The Faber Book of Science* design by Two Associates ¶ August 10: *Lake Wobegon Days* design by Paul Buckley, illustration by

Rodica Prato, *Yesterday's Houses* illustration by David Dean, *Summer Things* illustration by Simon Bartram, *Cooking with Fernet Branca* illustration by Marian Hill ¶ August 17: *Serious Concerns* design by Pentagram ¶ August 24: *A Grief Observed* design by Berthold Wolpe, author photo by Walter Stoneman, National Portrait Gallery London ¶ August 31: *Finnegans Wake* design by Wolpe ¶ September 7: *Woman in Mind* design by Pentagram, *Family Voices* image from edition published in 1981 by Next Editions, *The Caretaker* illustration by Andrzej Klimowski ¶ September 14: *Vernon God Little* cover design by Pentagram, *Ludmila's Broken English* design by Ghost, artwork © Burke/Triolo Productions ¶ September 21: *New Selected Poems 1957–1994* design by Pentagram ¶ September 28: *Family Matters* design by Pentagram, photo © 2000 Sooni Taraporevala, from her book *Parsis: a Photographic Journey*. Published by Good Books, Mumbai, India, *A Fine Balance* design by Darren Wall at Faber, photo © Dario Mitidieri ¶ October 5: *Memoir* design by Two Associates, *The Dark* design by Faber, photo by Michael Wildsmith/Millennium Images ¶ October 12: *Peacock Pie* illustration © Edward Ardizzone 1946 ¶ October 19: *Collected Poems* design by Pentagram ¶ October 26: *A Long Long Way* design by Two Associates, photo © Bettmann/Corbis, *Spies* design by Pentagram, photo by Michael Frayn, artwork by John Candell ¶ November 2: *Compost* design by Bertold Wolpe ¶ November 9: *Oscar and Lucinda* design by Pierre Le Tan, *True History of the Kelly Gang* design by Pentagram, photo courtesy of the State Library of New South Wales ¶ November 16: *Collected Poems 1909–1962* design by Pentagram ¶ November 23: *Sibelius* design by Bertold Wolpe, *Rip It Up and Start Again* cover design by Lotta Kühlhons ¶ November 30: *From an Abandoned Work* and *Waiting for Godot* designs by Faber ¶ December 7: *Lord of the Flies* design by Anthony Gross ¶ December 14: *Collected Poems* design by Pentagram ¶ December 21: Christmas card design and illustration by Barnett Freedman, reproduced by permission of the Freedman Estate ¶ December 28: *Venice* design by Tim Byrne, cover photo © Royalty Free/Corbis

Every effort has been made to contact copyright holders. In the event of an inadvertent omission, please write to the publishers at 3 Queen Square, London WC1N 3AU.

Faber Finds

Bringing great writing back into print

There can be few things more disheartening for an avid reader than to discover that your favourite book has gone out of print, or a much-loved author's work has become completely unavailable. Faber Finds is a groundbreaking new imprint whose aim is to restore to print for future generations a wealth of lost classics and authors of distinction.

Writers such as Wendy Cope, Julian Barnes and Michael Frayn have already chosen books they'd love to see published again, and now through our website everyone has the chance to nominate works to join the Faber Finds list.

Using the latest technology, the text of each book is beautifully reset and printed on high quality paper, with stunning cover designs generated by a unique computer program. When you order a copy your book is printed specially for you on demand.

You can explore the list and contribute your suggestions of great lost books at www.faberfinds.co.uk

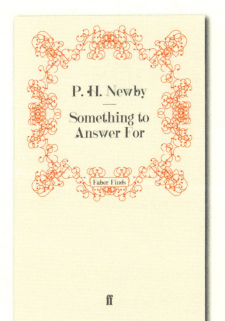
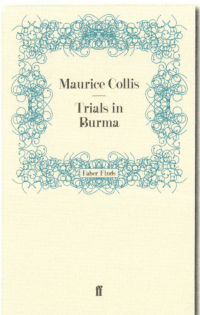
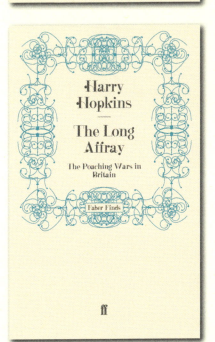
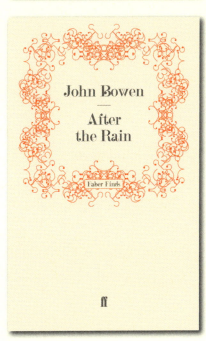

NOTES

NOTES

Win Eighty Faber Books!

As part of our eightieth-birthday celebrations we're offering eighty of our most celebrated and influential books as a prize to one lucky winner. A further twenty-five runners-up will receive prizes of the new *Illustrated Old Possum's Book of Practical Cats* by T. S. Eliot, illustrated by Axel Scheffler, which will be published in the autumn of 2009.

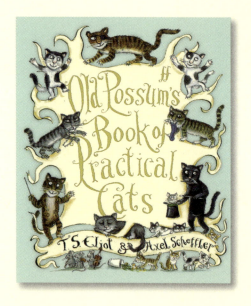

To enter all you need to do is visit www.faber.co.uk/diarycompetition and enter the answer to the question below along with your contact details.

The question:
Which Nobel Laureate published by Faber wrote *Death of a Naturalist* and *North*?

The closing date for entries is the 1 July 2009. For a full list of terms and conditions please see the website.